TRODDEN PATHS
A JOURNEY FROM BROOKFIELDS

BY

Modupe Broderick

EDITED BY WINSTON FORDE

Published by New Generation Publishing in 2022
Copyright © Modupe Broderick 2022

First Edition

The author asserts the moral right under the Copyright, Designs and Patents Act 1988 to be identified as the author of this work. All Rights reserved. No part of this publication may be reproduced, stored in a retrieval system, or transmitted, in any form or by any means without the prior consent of the author, nor be otherwise circulated in any form of binding or cover other than that which it is published and without a similar condition being imposed on the subsequent purchaser.

ISBN

    Paperback   978-1-80369-361-3
    Hardback   978-1-80369-362-0

www.newgeneration-publishing.com

 New Generation Publishing

Dedication

To the Memory of my Parents, Sylvester Modupe Broderick and Fernanda Gladys Nicol Broderick

Contents

Preface 1

PART ONE: ROOTS 7

Chapter 1 8

  A Province of Freedom on the West Coast of Africa 8

Chapter 2: 19

  My Father - Dr. Sylvester Modupe Broderick Sr. ... 19

Chapter: 3 24

  Fernanda Gladys Broderick, nee Nicol 24

Chapter: 4 32

  War Baby 32

Chapter: 5 35

  Me at Five Years - Exploring My neighbourhood, Being Mischievous, Discovering Relatives and Making Friends 35

Chapter: 6 41

  Formal Education in Sierra Leone From Kindergarten to Secondary School 41

Chapter: 7 62

  Life at 3, Main Motor Road Later at 17 Rasmusson Street. 62

Chapter: 8 71

  The Struggle for Independence - An Overview 71

PART TWO: NORTH AMERICA 74

Chapter: 9 75

  Sailing the Atlantic, North America Bound 75

Chapter: 10 82

  "In a Quiet Peaceful Village" 82

Chapter: 11 96
  "Quebec Oui, Ottawa Non" and "Vive le Quebec Libre." 96

Chapter: 12 111
  Greensboro - A Major Turning Point in my Academic Life 111

Chapter: 13 121
  "On Wisconsin" 121

PART THREE: FULL CIRCLE 130

Chapter: 14 131
  "Sannu da Zuwa" In the Land of the Emirs 131

Chapter: 15 140
  Baiacu, Itaparica Island, Bahia Brazil 140
  – An Interlude 140

Chapter: 16 151
  "Meme les Blancs Passent par Ici", Et "C'est Nous d'Abord qui Avons Vu les Blancs" 151

Chapter: 17 158
  The African Intelligentsia and Behaviours 158

APPENDICES 167

Appendix 1 - Classmates—Government Model School, 1949-52 (Standard 1-4) 168

Appendix 2 - Photographs 171

Appendix 3: Letter of Commendation on Modupe's performance at the USAID Regional Office – Abidjan (REDSO) 179

Appendix 4 - Bibliography 181

Preface

Trodden Paths: A Journey from Brookfields is inspired by a reflection that I prepared for my 50th graduation anniversary from Otterbein College (now Otterbein University) in late April 2013. For the occasion, the University authorities had requested members of the graduation class to prepare short essays describing their stories since graduation in 1963. Once the document was completed, I decided to do something similar for my father who had graduated from Otterbein in 1924. I thought it would be a fitting tribute to his memory and that a reflection of this nature, no matter how limited it was in scope, would serve as an introduction for my children and my sister's children to know something about their grandfather's life and his contribution to Education in Sierra Leone. On completion of the manuscript, I said to myself why not do reflections on my mother as she had played a critical role in the upbringing of my sister and me as well as other children of relatives and friends? In fulfilling this objective, I would leave for posterity narratives that portrayed the lives of two Sierra Leoneans (husband and wife) of the twentieth century; and which could serve as the basis for future research by Sierra Leoneans and non-Sierra Leonean scholars on several socio-historical topics.

The preparation of the manuscripts led me to interesting discoveries about my parents, which made me regret that I had not asked them more questions about their families. On the one hand, I realised that I had been handicapped by my not living in Sierra Leone during the twilight years of their lives as questions kept coming up during my sojourns in many African countries. On the other, as a child growing up, one is not yet knowledgeable or inquisitive enough to ask questions on family histories. Furthermore, there was always the risk of asking questions that parents deemed embarrassing and judged best left unanswered. However, based on the information gathered from both parents, I could say my father was not as forthcoming in talking about his relatives as had been my mother talking about hers. Indeed, I had obtained more information about my father's family from his older brother, my Uncle Dodd Broderick, than from any other member of his family. Indeed, I got the distinct impression that my father felt that some of these questions should not have been broached. I had taken the opportunity to ask my Uncle Dodd questions about the Broderick family while I was in Freetown conducting research for my Ph.D. dissertation in 1973. He was already in his late eighties, consequently his memory was not as good as it would have been had the interview been conducted in his seventies or early eighties. Another drawback pertained to my father's elder siblings, most of whom had died before I was born or were living outside of Sierra Leone as was the case of my Aunty Violet Broderick Boyle, who died in Enugu, Nigeria in 1977. I never had the opportunity of meeting her. Another elder sister of my father, Aunty Sarah Noah, nee Broderick, died in Calabar in the 1930s. I also regret not having taken the opportunity to talk with my Aunt Queenie Lewis, nee Broderick, my father's youngest sister, in whose house, the Broderick family house, (No. 6 Circular Road) my sister and I spent a lot of time during our childhood days. I could have also benefited from information provided by Auntie Queenie's children, my favourite first cousins, who were much older than me and would have been much more knowledgeable about my paternal grandmother. Although both of my parents lived long lives (my father died at 97 and my mother at 89), I concluded they may only have had limited knowledge of their families. For example, very late in my father's long life, I discovered that his childhood had not been happy. He had lost his father at age five, and it appeared to me that he was not comfortable talking about his immediate or extended family. Although he knew his mother very well, I do not recall him saying much about her either, despite being very fond of her. My mother lost her mother at age nine and her father was away from Freetown for most of her childhood, living on the far-away island of Fernando Po (now Bioko), where he was a Methodist Minister and plantation farmer. Her father had died when she was a student in England, in 1927. She was more knowledgeable about the maternal side of her family than her paternal relatives. In the sixties, she discovered her Parkinson relatives on her paternal side.

The completion of the manuscripts of both parents inspired me to initiate work on a manuscript reflecting on my own life. I was also motivated by my god brother, Henry Maduka Steady and by neighbourhood friend, John Edward Bankole Jones. Both were preparing manuscripts for their respective families. I thought I would do a manuscript on my life for three reasons: First, as mentioned above, to tell a story of my childhood experiences growing up in Freetown, so that my children, born and bred outside of Sierra Leone, and young Sierra Leoneans alike could get a glimpse of life of a middle-class boy growing up in the forties and fifties in Freetown. Second, to document my experiences as a student and teacher in North America and my growing social awareness; and third, to document my work experiences in Africa as an educator and a development expert.

This memoir is then a plea for more social histories of Sierra Leonean or African families and or personalities. It was undertaken to encourage Sierra Leoneans as well as African Scholars to carry out investigative research not only about their family histories or historical personalities but to investigate incidents that have impacted their professional lives. My twenty-six-year career working for an international development organisation in nine African countries and being a son of Africa, has equipped me with reflections that I would like to share, such as, my thoughts on the stumbling blocks that have affected development in Africa on the demand side (i.e., the assistance/products which African nations need from international donors to undertake development as well as the cultural behaviours of their citizens that hamper development). I emphasise the demand side because much has already been written on the supply side (technical assistance and products which donors provide to developing nations.) In addition, my concern for furthering on-going investigative research is triggered by the brutal civil unrests that plagued Liberia, Sierra Leone, and Cote d'Ivoire. These unrests resulted in the futile loss of several thousands of innocent lives that have negatively impacted the political and economic growth of these three African countries. Rather than blame colonialists for all our woes, thereby sweeping unhealthy African behaviours, which need to be addressed, under the rug and pretending they don't exist; my hope is to encourage rigorous analyses from the African intelligentsia to critically assess challenges and pinpoint the stumbling blocks that impede transformational development. An example of this type of investigative research is the article by the Honourable S.E. Osmond Hanciles, Deputy Minister 1, Sierra Leone's Ministry of Education, Science & Technology: *"Escaping the Mind Trap of our Village Attitude"*[1] This is a probing analysis that pinpoints some of the pitfalls plaguing nationhood in Sierra Leone. Another example of this type of analysis in a literary form is Omotunde Johnson's novel *"Dancing with Trouble."* I would contend that it is only when African leaders, scholars and the intelligentsia are committed to taking the bull by the horns to ask the hard questions and objectively identify common-sense solutions that are vetted through civil society, in a climate of lawfulness, security, transparency, and accountability, can they begin to lay the foundation for transformational development that will result in improvements in the quality of life of citizens.

I would like to express my gratitude to the following for their insightful thoughts and suggestions:

---

[1] Fwd: [SLPW] '3330 Article "Escaping the Mind Trap of our Village Attitude" Re; [fois] Youth Man Extraordinaire, October 7, 2013

Dr Devi Rajab, (former Dean of Students at the University of Natal, South Africa,) who read the first chapter of this manuscript in its infancy and recommended that I buttress my observations of personalities or events with narratives describing the socio-political or historical context of the times. Dr. Eugene Terry for his moral support and for providing critical feedback to improve sections of the manuscript, and my spouse Amelia Broderick who proofread the document and made valuable suggestions for its improvement, and my editor, Winston Forde, for meticulously copy-editing and proofreading my manuscript and explaining the intricate process of publishing. However, I take full responsibility for any factual errors or inaccuracies contained within the manuscript.

PART ONE: ROOTS

Chapter 1

A Province of Freedom on the West Coast of Africa

The founding of a Province of Freedom in 1787, on the west coast of Africa by the Black Poor from England, was an attempt by British abolitionists to terminate the Trans-Atlantic Slave Trade. The Black Poor comprised Africans who were living in England or African Americans who had fought on the side of the British during the American Revolutionary War and been rewarded freedom by migrating to England following the proclamation by Chief Justice Lord Mansfield, in the case involving James Somerset, an African American, who had been brought to England by his slave master, that slavery in England was illegal. [2] This experiment to eliminate the slave trade at the roots, specifically the Trans-Atlantic Slave Trade, would be later supported by the arrival of the so-called "Nova Scotians", in 1792 and the "Maroons" in 1800. The Nova Scotians were African American Loyalists, born in America or Africa, who were promised "freedom" in Canada by the British Government in exchange for their allegiance to the British Crown during the American Revolutionary War. The Maroons were Africans from Ghana who had revolted against their British masters in Jamaica and had been shipped to Nova Scotia from where they were repatriated to Sierra Leone. The repatriation of Liberated Africans or Recaptives, as they were also known to Sierra Leone, Liberia ("Congo People"), and other places on the west coast of Africa as a haven for freed slaves, intensified in the 1820s. The Liberated Africans comprised ethnic groups

---

[2]. "Somerset's Case," Wikipedia, last modified October 23, 2013, accessed October 23, 2013, http//en.wikipedia.org/wiki/Somersett%_case#

from as far north as Senegambia and as far south as Mozambique.[3] Their cultural and linguistic inputs together with similar inputs from local ethnic groups of Sierra Leone played a major role in shaping the Krio language and culture in Sierra Leone during the 19th and 20th centuries.

The concept of Creolization is not unique to Krio. It is a linguistic phenomenon that describes language divergence, i.e., when social contact generates the evolution of a third language triggered by trade and or conquest, etc. It used to be the custom of Sierra Leoneans to refer to the people as Creoles and the language as Krio. But this distinction has been rejected by present-day Krio scholars (Linguists and Historians) who used the term" Krio" to refer to both the people and their language. They argue that "Krio" is not a deformation of "Creole" as was usually thought, but an etymologically derived Yoruba word "Akiriyo", meaning those who walk around visiting or are involved in trading. Some Krio speakers, especially upper class, have had an ambivalent attitude toward their language, referring to it disparagingly as a "bastardisation" of English, as exemplified in Thomas Decker's satirical play, "Boss Coker Bifo Saint Peter". Because of this so-called "bastardisation", they refuse to speak Krio or do not consider it a valid language. Linguists, on the other hand, have demonstrated that Krio is a full fledge language with its own grammatical rules/patterns (Syntax), which show strong linguistic affinities with the Kwa linguistic subgroup of the Niger-Congo family of African languages, postulated by Joseph Greenberg. The Kwa linguistic grouping embraces coastal languages of West Africa extending from eastern Liberia to eastern Nigeria. This raises another question as to whether we should refer to Krio as an English based creole as some scholars do, when in fact its syntax is not English or Indo European. Furthermore, the syntax of Krio comprises serial verbs which are used to express a single

---

[3]. Sigismund Wilhelm Koelle, *Polyglotta Africana, AKADEMISCHE DRUCK-U. VERLAGSANSTALT, GRAZ-AUSTRIA*, 1963.

action, front focusing of verbs, idiophones, and the use of tone to differentiate lexical items, etc. - features which are common to languages of the Kwa linguistic group - unlike English. Furthermore, although English is a Germanic language, sixty percent of its vocabulary (lexicon) is from French, through the Norman Conquest; but we do not say English is "basterdise French", or a French based Creole, or that the Romance Languages are a "bastardisation" of Latin.

In England, the influence of French culture was significant until the end of the Middle Ages. French was the language of the courts, the language of discourse, the language of prestige, while English was considered a "beastial language. Yet despite this low-class classification, English is not considered a creole language, which indeed it is., according to the tenets of language divergence. Nor does the high percentage of French vocabulary make it a Romance Language. (i.e., languages derived from Latin: Italian, Spanish, Portuguese, French, and Romanian). Rather, English was considered a Germanic Language because of its structure.

Accordingly, Krio is not English, it has never been English, it was never spoken by the English. Rather, it is an African Based Creole just like Lingala, Ki-Tuba, Sango, Afrikaans, and Ki-Swahili, which is a Bantu language, - although a significant amount of Ki-Swahili's lexicon is from Arabic. Based on language divergence, through migration, trade and conquest, some Linguists argue that all languages are Creoles.[4]

The Nova Scotians and Maroons further reinforced Christian influence. The Nova Scotians, known as "settlers", a term that was later extended to embrace the Maroons, shared similar origins with their Black Poor brethren whose arrival in 1787 initiated the repatriation experiment. They, for the most part, had succumbed to

---

[4] For a detailed discussion of the terms "Creole/Krio", please see Gibril Cole's work, "The Krio of West Africa," and Akintola Wyse's," Krio of Sierra Leone: An Interpretive History."

Christianity while in North America. Methodists by faith, the Nova Scotians and Maroons built the first churches in central Freetown: Zion Wilberforce Street, Rawdon Street Chapel, Wesley Church, Ebenezer Church, St John Maroon Church and Gibraltar Church and Zion on the Hill (Wesley Street). On the other hand, the Anglican Church, through its Church Missionary Society (CMS), supported English and German religious scholars in their efforts to study the linguistic aspects of African languages for translating the Bible. They believe that linguistic knowledge of these languages was vital for converting Africans to Christianity. Freetown was thus a haven for this experiment as the presence of a very large body of Liberated or repatriated Africans presented these scholars with the opportunity to fulfil their mission. Later the British Government would intensify its role in trying to convert Africans from their local traditions and or Islamic faith to Christianity both in Sierra Leone and along the West African coast, although Islam was already present in West Africa prior to the arrival of Christian Missionaries.

Liberated Africans' contributions to the area that would later become Nigeria have been well documented by numerous scholars on both sides of the Atlantic. For example, Jean Herskovits Kopytoff's work, "A Preface to Modern Nigeria - The Sierra Leoneans in Yoruba 1830-1890," [5] has become a classic reference for understanding the multi-faceted contributions, starting with Bishop Crowder's Niger Mission. Liberated Africans' contributions, both Christian and Muslim, were significant in creating African colonial elites, especially in Christian missionary work, education and administration, during the nineteenth century in the homeland of their forefathers, particularly the area that became known as Nigeria. This input by Sierra Leoneans, "Saros", as they were

---

[5]. Jean Herskovits Kopytoff, *A Preface to Modern Nigeria: Sierra Leoneans in Yoruba, 1830-1890.* Madison: University of Wisconsin Press, 1965.

affectionately known in Nigeria, extends from as far north as Senegambia to as far south as Angola[6].

As far as I know, my family (Broderick and Nicol) does not have direct kinship ties with the Nova Scotians or Maroons, but rather with principally Yoruba culture for both of my parents and Popo culture on my mother's side.[7] My family also has ethnic ties with Sierra Leone and the Gambia through the Sherbro of southwestern Sierra Leone and the Wolof of Senegambia[8]. On the Yoruba side of my mother, I'm one of the great grandsons of the Venerable Archdeacon George, James, Macauley of the Church Missionary Society (CMS) Anglican Church[9]. He was the first Sierra Leonean to serve as an archdeacon of the diocese and had been educated at the Sierra Leone Grammar School founded by the Church Missionary Society in 1845. He was from the Yoruba subgroups: Egba and Ijesha. His marriage to my great grandmother, whose name I do not know,

---

[6] For a detailed description of the role played by Islam in fashioning Creole/Krio Society in the region, please see Gibril Cole's work, *The Krio of West Africa*, Athens, Ohio University Press, 2013.

[7] The Popos are located on the coastal region of the present-day Republic of Benin.

[8] Since starting this autobiography, I have taken the Ancestry DNA test. The results confirm my strong West African roots. I am 95% African which breaks down as follows:

53% Nigerian

23% Benin/Togo,

7% Ivory Coast/Ghana

5% Mali

5% Senegal

2% Africa South Central.

The remaining 5% breaks down as follows: 3% Europe East and 2% West Asia

[9] George James Macauley, Sierra Leone, Anglican (CMS), accessed October 24, 2013,
http://www.dacb.org/stories/sierraleone/macauley_georgejames html

produced my grandmother, Gladys Macauley and her siblings.

Yoruba culture on my father's side derives from my great grandfather, my father's grandfather, who is buried in the village cemetery of Wellington, now part of greater Freetown. He produced three children, two sons and one daughter. His eldest child was William Archibald Broderick who married a Mariah Shaw of Sherbro and European origin through the Tucker family of Gbap[10]. The union produced eleven children of whom eight lived. My father was the sixth child of those who lived from this union, and two elder sisters, Aunty Sarah Broderick and Aunty Violet Broderick married Sierra Leoneans who went to Nigeria to work and where they eventually died. Aunty Sarah married a Noah of the Noah family of Sawpit and died in Calabar in the 1930s and Aunty Violet married Reverend Boyle. She died in Enugu in 1977. Their only son, Samuel Modupe Boyle, married Josephine, Modupeh, Eliza Scott from Hastings village and produced five children who hyphenated their names to Scott-Boyle: Archibald Ola Scott-Boyle, Shirley Scott-Boyle (now Mrs. Rogers-Wright,) Meredith Scott-Boyle, Victor Scott-Boyle and Rita Scott-Boyle (now Mrs. Johnson). My father's other older sister, Aunty Nora, never married. My father's two older brothers worked in Nigeria. Uncle Dodd Broderick worked in Jos with a mining company and following retirement

---

[10] The Tuckers are an Afro-European clan of Sherbro ancestry from the Southern region of Sierra Leone. Their progeny, it is claimed, stems from an English trader and agent, John Tucker, and a Sherbro princess. From the 17th Century, the Tuckers ruled over the most powerful Sherbro chiefdoms of Southern Sierra Leone, centred on the village of Gbap.
Observation: It should be noted, however, that my Ancestry DNA results do not show a genetic link with Sierra Leone. The closest it comes to Sierra Leone is with Mali and Senegal. The attribution with Sherbro ethnicity needs further investigation.
From Wikipedia, Sherbro Tuckers

returned to Sierra Leone. Uncle Dodd produced two issues with his common law wife Amelia Jones: Dr. Nathaniel Ade Broderick and Kunle Broderick. Uncle Dodd's younger brother, Uncle Sonny Broderick whom my father followed in the order of birth, worked in Lagos and died there. I do not know whether he had issues. My father and his siblings had an older stepbrother (William Broderick, affectionately referred to as Brother Willy) who also worked and died in Nigeria. He had offspring in Sierra Leone (Ojo Broderick and Jowo Broderick), and probably in Nigeria. Given this Nigerian connection, I have often wondered whether the former Nigerian Junior Eagles coach, Sebastian Brodericks, is a descendant of the Brodericks from Sierra Leone. My grandfather also had children out of wedlock that my father did not talk about. Only Uncle Dodd and Aunty Queenie had mentioned them in passing. For example, Arthur Broderick, a half-brother, became acting mayor of Freetown in the early sixties. When I lived in Liberia, I met Brodericks who hailed from Sinoe County and some claimed origins from Sierra Leone and from the village of Wellington—probably my relatives.

My father's uncle, Ebenezer, O'Callaghan, Broderick (EOB), who lived in Wilberforce and whom we called "Grandpa" as opposed to "Grand Uncle", had two female issues (Kezia Broderick, named after his sister, and Dolly Broderick) from his marriage to a Miss Maxwell. "Grandpa" also worked in Nigeria. Aunty Kezia married Mr. Lenrie Peters, (it is claimed a descendant of Thomas Peters of the Nova Scotians) and they settled in the Gambia. They had five children, (Mrs. Bijou Bidwell, nee Peters, Dr. Florence Asie Mahoney, nee Peters (Ph.D. Historian), Dr. Lenrie Peters (Medical Doctor and Writer), Ms. Ruby Peters (United Nations administrator), and Mr. Dennis Alaba Peters—Actor and BBC Broadcaster).

My father had returned to Sierra Leone from the United States in 1928 and my mother had returned from England also that same year. Unfortunately, I do not have any information on how they met nor about their courtship. But given that Freetown is a small city, it should not have been difficult for them to meet. Four years later they were married on Easter Sunday at the Saint George's Cathedral. The union produced two issues: Sylvester Modupe Broderick Jr. and Ore Awoonor Renner, nee Broderick). Sylvester (Modupe) married Amelia Fitzjohn and had two issues: Vania, Ayodele, Lesana, Broderick and Ahovi Fitzjohn Modupe Broderick. Vania married Ismael Dursun (a Turkish-American) and that union produced a daughter, Zara, Ayodele Dursun and son, Troy Broderick Dursun. Ore Broderick married Walter Awoonor Renner and had three issues: Lauris Awoonor Renner, Julian Awoonor Renner and Liesel Awoonor Renner. My father's younger brother, Robert Broderick, did not have issues as far as I know. If he did, no member of the Broderick family mentioned them to me. My father's youngest sister, Queenie, Maria, Broderick, married Samuel Lewis and that union produced six children of whom four lived: Omotunde Elizabeth Baiete-Williams, nee Lewis, Ebun Violet Porter, nee Lewis, Sylvester Olufemi Archibald Lewis, and Dennis, Emrick, Tamawo, Lewis. They all grew up in the family house on 6 Circular Road in Freetown. Little did I know that someday I would continue the Broderick tradition of working in Nigeria - first as a University Lecturer and second as an International Development Expert.

While living in Nigeria, first in the North and later in the South, I met several Nigerians of Sierra Leonean descent. The first occasion took place at Bayero University in Kano where I met students who had relatives in Freetown. These students sought me out to discuss their families when they found out that I was from Sierra Leone. And I knew some of their families. Also, in Kano, I met the famous Walker family who had lived there for many years and whose offspring spoke Krio very well. I also recall a visit of a young female Nigerian student from Lagos to Bayero University whose name I have unfortunately forgotten. She was informed by students of a Sierra Leonean lecturer on campus. The student sought me out and during our meeting we conversed in Krio. She had never touched foot on Sierra Leonean soil and had learned her Krio from her parents— one parent hailed from Hastings and the other from Murray Town. Her Krio was excellent—full of idiomatic expressions. I remarked that with such an excellent command of Krio intonation, Freetonians would consider her funny in the head had she found herself in that city asking for directions to principal landmarks. While working in Lagos, I also met several Nigerians with Sierra Leonean roots, Adeniyi-Jones, Lukes, Rhodes, members of the Ransome-Kuti family, Shitta-Bey, Johnson, Coker, etc. I also had a cousin (Muriel Okagbwe, nee Maxwell) who had married Mr. Okagbwe, a Nigerian businessman and lived on Victoria Island. I had several visits with her and with her mother, Aunty Araba, during my sojourn in Lagos. In the Republic of Benin, I had the good fortune of visiting the King of Ketu at his royal seat of power in the town of Ketu, the ancestral home of my paternal great grandfather who is buried in the village of Wellington. I was greeted with cheering sounds from women who called out my name Modupe Ooooo. I was led to the King's court where I was received. I was nervous as I knelt before the King who placed his hands on my head and welcomed me. I felt like a prodigal son. Although the King spoke French, protocol demanded that he addressed his visitors in Yoruba. After completing his welcoming remarks in Yoruba, he told me in French he was aware of his ancestors' offspring living in various countries in the New World as well as in countries on the West African coast. I then thanked the King for receiving me, shook his hands and prepared to leave, overwhelmed by the visit and its significance. I would later conclude it was significant in that my knowledge of my great grandfather's origins, had enabled me to physically reconnect with his birthplace-- one of my ancestral roots. Years later with the advent of DNA testing, the Ketu narrative has added value to the link confirming my historical roots and relatives with my DNA ethnicity. My DNA results show a 53% link with Nigeria, and a 23% link with Benin and Togo. My paternal great grandfather, a Yoruba Liberated African and progenitor of the Brodericks, had probably landed in Sierra Leone in the 1820s from Ketu on a slave ship. He probably was baptised by a Christian missionary and given the surname Broderick or adopted it from his master/patron or from a foreigner with whom he was close. After receiving my DNA results, a fourth Cousin, Walton Gilpin, a Sierra Leonean who lives in Texas, contacted me as there was a high match with Broderick in his results. (There was also a high match with Gilpin in my results.) He told me that his family tree showed a relation with the Brodericks but did not know the connection. I was able to confirm that we were related through Sally Hughes, one of my father's first cousins who was an offspring of Kezia Broderick, daughter of the Broderick patriarch from Ketu and my father's aunt. Kezia Broderick married a Reverend Hughes from Bonthe, who worked in the Gambia. That union produced five children of which Sally Hughes was the eldest. She married William Gilpin and that union produced Buck Gilpin who is the father of Walton Gilpin. Thus, Walton Gilpin and I are both descendants from the Broderick patriarch Ketu (my great grandfather) through Kezia Broderick mother of Sally Hughes.

My Beninese secretary for the International Organisation for which I worked in Cotonou turned out to be the first cousin of my friend Ahovi Kponou. When she discovered my Sierra Leonean heredity, she told me the story of her uncle, her father's older brother, Mr. Andre Kponou, who had gone to Sierra Leone where he had married a Sierra Leonean woman (Mary Easmon) and had not returned to Benin. Initially, I did not make the link with the Kponou family as the way she pronounced the name in Fon or Goun was very different from the way the name is pronounced in Sierra Leone. When she wrote the name down, I immediately made the connection. The next day she brought me photographs of the wedding of her cousin Kathleen Kponou, Ahovi's younger sister, to Joseph Ashwood, a schoolmate of mine. Indeed, the photographs had pictures of my sister and my wife who had been bridesmaids.

Going through the Register of Old Boys of the Sierra Leone Grammar School and the Prince of Wales School, my Alma Mater, I discovered several past pupils with the surname Broderick. I would venture to say that all Brodericks who attended the Sierra Leone Grammar School are descendants of my paternal great grandfather. The Brodericks on the Register for the Prince of Wales are probably my relatives as well, but I do not know how they might be related to me.

Chapter 2:

My Father - Dr. Sylvester Modupe Broderick Sr.

My father, Papa as we called him, was born on June 13, 1893, at Lower Commissariat in Freetown, Sierra Leone, an area in central Freetown where the former Labour Office was located. Following its demolition in the early sixties, a new building was erected on the site that would later house the old American Embassy. His father, a clerk in the Sierra Leone military offices on Tower Hill, worshipped at Holy Trinity Church, where he was an usher. At age five he lost his father and to ease the financial burden on his mother, who had to provide for the other children, he and his younger brother, Robert, were sent to live with their paternal grandmother and cousins in his father's village of Wellington. There, they attended primary school and partook in church activities at the village Anglican Church. He suffered an injury to his left eye, during his youth, and eventually lost his sight in that eye. After completing primary school, he attended the Albert Academy, founded in 1904 by American missionaries of the United Brethren Church UBC (now United Methodist), and there he completed his secondary schooling in 1912. He was a schoolmate of the Tuboku-Metzger brothers, Constance and Samuel - the former taught Science for years at the Prince of Wales School and would become the school's first Sierra Leonean Principal. He later served as Sierra Leone's Ambassador to Liberia. The latter, who also taught at the Prince of Wales, founded the Faremi Workshop, a furniture company located at Kissy Road in Freetown. All three of them would later find themselves in the United States of America, where they completed first and second university degrees. On completing the Albert Academy, Papa taught at the Evangelical United Brethren (EUB) Primary Mission

School at Rotifunk and had students such as John Karefa–Smart, a future Otterbein graduate, class of 1940, and later Sierra Leone's first Foreign Minister. Through the EUB Mission, he entered Otterbein College (now Otterbein University) in 1920, located in Westerville, Ohio in the United States of America. To obtain his full passage to America from Sierra Leone, he travelled as a working passenger on the New Brunswick, which docked at Ellis Island in New York City on August 02, 1920,[11] and to defray his college tuition and other expenses, he did odd jobs on campus and in the town of Westerville. He was the second Sierra Leonean to attend Otterbein University and the first to graduate. The first Sierra Leonean to attend Otterbein was Joseph Hannibal Caulker, who tragically died in a fire accident in 1900, his senior year. My father excelled in his studies and graduated with honours (cum laude) in 1924. He was a long-distance runner and won a gold watch for his athletic achievements. After Otterbein, he attended Columbia University (Teachers College) in New York City and completed a master's degree in Education in 1926. He taught for two years at North Carolina Agricultural and Technical State University in Greensboro and returned to Sierra Leone in 1928 to take up an appointment as an Inspector of Schools with the Education Department of the Sierra Leone British Colonial Government. It was not an easy situation in those colonial days for Africans who had received degrees from American Universities, as they had to demonstrate in so many ways that they were as competent as their British trained counterparts - both British and African. The British Government frowned on American degrees and adopted a policy that required African graduates of American Universities to take what they deemed as "remedial courses" in British Universities prior to or after an appointment. From the position of Inspector of Schools, he

---

[11]. "Ellis Island-Free Port of New York Passenger Records Search," accessed March 7, 2013,
http://www.ellisisland.org/search/viewTextManifest,asp?MID=1 5554...

rose to become Assistant Director of Education, the second Sierra Leonean to hold that position, the first having been Reverend Charles Macaulay, an Oxford trained Sierra Leonean graduate and the husband of Mrs. Agnes Smythe-Macaulay. The position of Assistant Director of a department was the highest an African could hold during the colonial period. For his services to the British Colonial Government of Sierra Leone, he was honoured by His Majesty's Government in 1947 with the medal, "Officer of the British Empire (OBE)."

Following retirement, Papa served in various educational and managerial capacities including being the Acting Principal of the Sierra Leone Grammar School and Registrar for External Exams. He also served as a manager of the Freetown Mineral Water Company, which bottled soft drinks, produced, and sold bread, and offered recreational facilities and entertainment space to the public. In 1953, he obtained a Fulbright Fellowship from the U.S. Department of State and served as a Visiting Professor at Northwestern University in Evanston, Illinois, where he lectured on African Studies in a programme directed by Melville Herskovits. In 1959, he received a second Fulbright Fellowship, which took him to North Carolina Agricultural and Technical College in Greensboro, North Carolina where he lectured for two years before returning to Sierra Leone. His third Fulbright Professorship took him to Western College for Women in Oxford, Ohio, and later to North Carolina Agricultural and Technical State University. Otterbein University, his alma mater, awarded him an honorary Doctor of Humane Letters Degree in 1947 and with the Distinguished Alumnus Award in 1961.

Papa was very energetic in many activities: education, sports, scouting and social. He was a member of the Fourah Bay College (now University of Sierra Leone) Council, on which he served for many years. He was Vice President of the Sierra Leone Football Association and would later become its President. At an earlier period, he had been a referee of the Football Association (soccer). He was the

President of the Wellington Descendant's Association whose members lobbied the Government for better conditions and facilities for their village. As a child, I vividly recall trips to Wellington to visit his home village and attending the annual Thanksgiving Memorial Service held at the village Anglican Church. He was one of the founding fathers of the Freetown Dinner Club, a social group in which he actively participated. He hardly missed an opportunity to attend the club's monthly dinners held on the second Saturday. The Freetown Dinner Club had started during the colonial period to promote better relationships between senior Sierra Leoneans civil servants and their British colonial counterparts. He was also a stalwart supporter of the Albert Academy Old Boys Association and played a significant role in the school's welfare. At his funeral, the Old Boys Association and present-day pupils were present in full force to honour their oldest old boy. A tribute was paid at his wake honouring his service to the School by Mr. Max Bailor, the Principal and, himself, a former Otterbein University graduate—class of 1953. The old boys and present-day pupils lustily sang the school song as his remains were laid to rest.

Papa was also active in scouting and became Chief Scout of Sierra Leone. He also served for several years on the Board of Trustees of the Freetown Secondary School for Girls and was its chairman for several years, a role now being fulfilled by his daughter, Mrs. Ore Awoonor-Renner. To honour his services to his country, a Primary School was established in his name on Fergusson Street in the western side of Freetown. On his retirement from the Sierra Leone Government in 1950, he was appointed a member of the Freetown City Council, a position that he held for several years. He took the opportunity to visit Otterbein University for the last time in 1976 and while there; he proudly wore his track sweater showing off the Big O. He was warmly received by Dr DeVore, the University President, and by Mr. Bud Yeost, the Director of the Athletic Department.

Papa was in good health all his life. Even in his eighties he regularly took his walks (which he referred to as "constitution walks",) which took him from his residence at Rasmusson Street to King Harman Road, to Merewether Road (now Jomo Kenyatta Road), to Pademba Road, to Campbell Street, to St. John, to Savage Street, to Main Motor Road and finally back to Rasmusson St, a circuit of about six miles. He continued driving his old Ford Consul (licence plate F 9028) well into his nineties until the Sierra Leone Police stopped him from doing so. Papa was good friends with Dr. Isaac Chiakazia Steady, Sir Emile Fashole Luke, Mr. Sam Johnson, Constance Tuboku-Metzger, Samuel Tuboku- Metzger, Mr. Arthur O. Stuart, Sir Ernest Morgan, Sir Ernest Beoku-Betts, Mr. Kenneth Fergusson (Sr.), Reverend Melville Cole, Mr. Akiwande Akiwumi, Mr. Jacob Lewis (Druggist), Dr. S.M. Renner, Mr. Kingston King, Mr. C.S. Bankole Terry, Dr. Arthur (Tot) Boyle-Hebron, Dr. W H Fitzjohn, etc. He died peacefully in his sleep at the grand old age of 97 on October 20, 1990. For his services to his country, he was honoured with a state funeral, attended by Joseph Saidu Momoh, the President of Sierra Leone. He was interred at the Racecourse Cemetery, on the east side of Freetown, where his mother and other relatives are buried.

Chapter: 3

Fernanda Gladys Broderick, nee Nicol

My mother, Mama as we called her, was born on April 09, 1904, at Goree Street on the east side of Freetown. She was the daughter of the Reverend William Fergusson Nicol, a Methodist Minister, and Gladys Macauley. Her father was named in honour of William Fergusson, a Jamaican who became the first black governor of Sierra Leone. He was very well liked by Sierra Leoneans and served twice in this capacity. Her father was a Methodist missionary on the island of Fernando Po, now Bioko, and a part of Equatorial Guinea, where he became a cocoa-plantation farmer at San Carlos, now Luba. He was among the many Sierra Leonean families who worked on the island as teachers, administrators, missionaries, entrepreneurs, and plantation owners, during the 19th and 20th centuries. In addition to Sierra Leoneans, there were also Liberians, Ghanaians, Nigerians, and Cameroonians, who worked on the island as labourers.

Mama was the granddaughter of the venerable George James Macauley, the first African Archdeacon of the Church Missionary Society of the Anglican Church in Sierra Leone. She had a younger sister, named Rosaline, who died at age five. She also had an older sister (Auntie Etta) but from a different mother. Her mother died when she was nine. Her father remarried but did not always reside in Freetown; she was raised by her stepmother, whose name, unfortunately, I do not know.

Mama attended primary school at the Cathedral School and secondary school at the Annie Walsh Memorial School for Girls. After completing her secondary schooling, her father sent her to the United Kingdom in 1921 to study secretarial work at Pittman's College in London. Her father died in Fernando Po, in 1927, while she was still a student in England. In spite of her intense sorrow, she successfully completed her studies and returned home in 1928. She worked as a secretary for a period with Elder Dempster Lines Ltd.

Mama was a very industrious, determined and agriculturally-minded woman. She was blessed with a business mind, a genetic trait that she probably inherited from her father. This genetic trait is also evident in other descendants of his, (for example, Nigel Parkinson, who owns a successful construction company in Washington DC, and his sister, Verona Parkinson, who is a successful farmer in Mozambique, are both descendants, through their mother, Faith Parkinson, of my maternal grandfather, William Ferguson Nicol. Mama had the habit of saying to her children, "Business pays. You must not look down on business" or "nothing ventured, nothing gained." My earliest recollection of her business acumen dates from the mid-forties when she started a bakery at our residence on 14 King Harman Road in Brookfields. I later discovered that the bakery had started before I was born while she and Papa lived at 29 Pultney Street in central Freetown. When the family moved to the residence on King Harman Road in 1944, I vividly remember her bakers kneading the dough and putting the kneaded dough into baking pans that went into a coal pot-heated oven. People in the Brookfields' neighbourhood would come to our residence with large baskets to buy bread for resale. As for us, the residents of the house, we had a constant supply of freshly baked bread to eat just about every day. She continued with her bakery until the late forties when she was stricken with a case of double pneumonia. Upon her recovery, she was advised by her doctor, Radcliff Jones, not to continue with the bakery – (much to her chagrin) as the demands from its management had been injurious to her health. She was treated with penicillin whose wonders she touted for the rest of her life. Later in life, she was stricken with a severe case of arthritis and was hospitalised. After two weeks, she returned home not fully recovered. Dr. John Karefa-Smart then treated her with a drug that brought her almost immediate relief, and as she continued with the medication, she completely regained her health. She would remark, "Dr. Smart is very smart indeed." This experience further boosted her confidence in North American trained professionals.

Undeterred by these health setbacks, she undertook other business adventures. With the earnings that she had made, she bought a 16-acre farm in the late forties in Goderich, a seaside village on the western side of the Sierra Leone peninsular. On the farm, she raised pigs and became a regular supplier of pork to the Cold Storage Company in Freetown. She also raised vegetables and chickens, which her family consumed and would share with our neighbours and friends. Following this activity, she entered the exporting business, concentrating on bananas. She travelled to Newton, Songo, Marampa, Bradford, Rotifunk, Lunsar, Bauya, and Moyamba where she bought unripe bananas and had them sent to her cousin's residence, Mrs. Ayo Lew Wray, (nee Macauley) on Rawdon Street. There, the bananas were wrapped in brown paper and prepared for shipping abroad in cardboard boxes. On another occasion, she had rice grown in an empty area not far from our residence on Rasmusson Street. The yield from the rice-growing venture amounted to six bags. Following her agricultural undertaking, she bought a tipper truck and became a supplier of stones (crushed rocks) and sand to building contractors.

Mama was also gifted with her hands. She capitalised on this skill by becoming a talented seamstress. She made clothes for me (up to the end of my primary school days), my sister, and for herself. She sewed with a manual Singer machine that had been given to her by her father while she was a student in England. In addition to clothes making, she also made covers for settees. One of her clients was Mrs. Beresford-Stokes, the wife of the Governor of Sierra Leone for whom she made several settee covers. Using a manual sewing machine for such elaborate work caused a lot of physical discomfort to the arm and shoulder. Thus, she upgraded the manual machine to an electric unit with the proceeds she had acquired. She also made settee covers for friends and one such person was the Reverend Alice Fitzjohn, who would later become my mother-in-law. To complement her dressmaking skills, she had my father, who was in America, send her belt making materials. To attract customers, she advertised her products in the Daily Mail, the principal newspaper of the day. She would make belts, and buckles; and to promote customer service, she offered clients the choice of deciding on the width of the belt and the design of the buckles. She was also a pioneer in her dressing and was probably the first woman of her age group to don a pantsuit in a society that was known for its conservative values. Unfortunately, her sewing machines, which had given her financial satisfaction, were stolen in the early seventies from her residence on Rasmusson Street. Of great emotional loss was the machine that had been given her by her father. She was good friends of Ms. Miranda Coker of Kissy Road and later of Fourah Bay Road, who was a renowned seamstress in Freetown in the forties and fifties, and very active in Young Women Christian Association (YWCA) affairs. She would visit with her on a regular basis to discuss dressmaking and women's social issues.

Mama also had a discerning eye for perfection. Often when I would have a safari suit or shirt made by a local tailor, she would note, "the sleeves are not hanging correctly, one side is further down than the other, the buttons are not correctly placed. I need to correct that." She would remove the sleeves from the jacket, do a refitting on me, using pins to make sure the sleeves or buttons were rightly placed, and then do the re-stitching. Her penchant for having items being prim and proper was also evident in her shining brass trays, which decorated the walls of her living room or her shining floors. As a child, she had me clean these items on a regular basis with brick dust and lime.

Mama was very active in women's affairs. For example, she played a dynamic role in the YWCA and was chairperson of its Property Committee. She was full of ideas and a good conversationalist. Through her influence, the YWCA acquired land directly behind our house on Rasmusson Street on which they erected a boarding school for girls. The erection of this building on tennis courts on which we had played as children caused my father much displeasure as it was too close for his comfort. In 1973 when I returned to Sierra Leone to undertake field research for my Ph.D. dissertation, I commented on the closeness of the building, which triggered this remark from my father, "Our privacy is gone. It's all due to Mama. We have lost our privacy because she brought a school to our backyard." When we moved from King Harman Road to Main Motor Road in 1950, there were only five houses on that street, ours became the sixth. Open spaces studded with trees and shrubs comprised the rest of the area. As the fifties went by, more houses were built on these open spaces. The growth reflected the changing dynamics of urbanisation in Freetown - as new houses were now being built in the western area of the city, away from the congested east and central areas. But I never thought the powers that be would have erected a building on the Freetown City Council Tennis Courts.

Through the YWCA, Mama was able to bring women together to address women's issues and to undertake well-meaning activities for children. For example, on New Year's Day, the YWCA organised picnics for school children at Lumley Beach where they would be treated to jollof rice (a delicacy prepared for special occasions) and other delicious food items (cake, rice bread, ginger beer, ginger cake, coconut cake and groundnut cake). In addition, she was also very interested in the political situation of the fifties and she and her friends regularly attended Legislative Council meetings to hear discussions on the debate for self-governance, which led to independence in 1961. On other occasions, she and her friends would organise tea parties where they discussed contemporary social issues and children's affairs. Her concern for the disadvantaged became a "cause celebre" for the young. She probably developed this compassion from having been a stepchild who had lost her biological mother at an early age and was raised by a stepmother. During her lifetime, there were several young people who lived with us and who were educated by her. One of them, Joseph, Lisa, Tommy, attended the Prince of Wales with me and later became a Professor of Agriculture at Ngala University following the completion of his Ph.D. at Michigan State University in the United States of America. Through her connection with my future father-in-law, Dr. William H Fitzjohn, Charge d'Affaires at the Sierra Leone Embassy in Washington DC, she was able to seek his assistance to obtain scholarships for promising students to attend American Universities, One such beneficiary was Dr. James Funna, former World Bank employee, who graduated from Lincoln University in Pennsylvania and completed his Ph.D. studies at Tufts University's Fletcher School of Diplomacy.

In the sixties, she accompanied her husband, who was a visiting Fulbright Scholar, on two visits to the United States, and in the seventies, she visited with Amelia Fitzjohn (who would later become my wife) and her mother (Alice Fitzjohn) in Washington DC. Following her visit to Washington DC, she visited me at the University of Wisconsin-Madison. I remember holding a reception for her to which my professors and student friends were invited. I had just been awarded my Ph.D. degree from the Department of African Languages and Literature and was getting ready to take up an appointment as a Senior Lecturer at Bayero University in Kano in Northern Nigeria.

Her visits to America had a big impact on her. She was impressed by the generosity of Americans who entertained her in their homes and by the large variety of food available on such occasions or the abundance of food at students' cafeteria. She was also impressed with American technological success: its largeness, starting with the large shopping malls, the architecture of buildings, the amenities in their homes, their manicured farms and large cattle, the width of the roads and the size and number of wheels on a truck. She would remark, "That lorry has twenty wheels."

Mama believed in running a disciplined and organised home. She was fond of saying, "Serving your home is serving the Lord." She took great pride in keeping her home in an upright manner and made sure that her children acquired the requisite house-keeping skills. Accordingly, she was a strict but fair disciplinarian; and we (children) were never spoiled. At an early age, she taught me how to clean my room, make my bed, wash dishes and pots and pans, do the laundry and ironing, clean the bathroom, and paint the interior to upgrade the house, as well as how to cook and bake. Concerned about her religious upbringing, she made my sister and I attend biblical studies on Friday afternoons at the Cathedral School on a regular basis. She was also an avid gardener and took pride in maintaining a lovely garden at her residence. During the dry season, we children would water the flowers with hoses that she had bought. Her tightly knit organisation qualities could be noticed in every room, causing my father to observe, "Mama has taken everywhere in the house. There is no space left for us." She decorated the yard by growing a variety of flowers and fruit trees: star apples, mangoes, local apples, bananas, pawpaw, sugar cane, etc. She also reinforced her gardening interests by becoming a stalwart member of the Horticultural Society of Freetown. Her gardening partner was Mrs. Millie Betts, wife of Sir Ernest Beoku-Betts, who maintained a first-class garden at her residence in Congo Valley. No doubt, my sister, Mrs. Ore Awoonor-Renner inherited her gardening and business skills. She runs a successful floral business from flowers grown in her garden at her residence on Signal Hill Road.

Mama lived a long life and, except for bouts with pneumonia, malaria, and arthritis, was in relatively good health. She was a kind and generous person who had a strong love for the land and, had she been given the support, would have achieved more in her entrepreneurial endeavours. She strongly believed in her Christian faith and tried to live by its principles. She loved people and music, enjoyed cooking and entertaining, and hosted guests from home and abroad. In her eighties, she would still make sweets such as rice bread, groundnut and ginger cake for her grandchildren and guests. She also made the best ginger beer that I have ever had. Through her vision and hard work, she was able to complement her husband in many ways. Due to her foresight, she was responsible for acquiring extra land on which the family house was built on Rasmusson Street, acquiring property in Wilberforce Village in the thirties and acquiring land at Goderich Village in the late forties. Regarding her father's property on Bioko (Fernando Po), which she visited on several occasions, she occasionally received proceeds. But due to the political upheaval that took place on the island in the seventies, she and her stepsister's relatives may have lost claim to their father's plantation. Ironically, her land at Goderich was also lost to land poachers during the Sierra Leone civil war in the nineties.

My last vivid recollection of her took place at the time of my father's death in October 1990. She sat in her favourite corner of the dining room calmly playing the game of Snakes and Ladders with her granddaughter, Liesel Awoonor-Renner, as sympathisers called to offer condolences. She died on March 29, in 1993, a few days short of her eighty-ninth birthday. She was interred at Racecourse Cemetery next to her husband, who had preceded her in death three years earlier at age ninety-seven.

Chapter: 4

War Baby

I was a war baby, born on September 15, 1941, almost exactly two years after the start of the Second World War on September 1, 1939. Sierra Leone, a British colony, as well as other British colonies and territories in Africa, Asia and the Caribbean, had been drawn into the war, due to their colonial status, to provide infantry and logistical support to Great Britain's war efforts in Europe and Asia. Freetown's natural harbour became a sanctuary to British naval and commercial vessels, totalling over a hundred that were anchored at the estuary of the Sierra Leone River. Schools and government buildings were commissioned as offices and hostels, and several civil servants of the Government of Sierra Leone, including my father, served as Air Raid Precaution Wardens. They were tasked with providing information on sheltering and first aid assistance to civilians in the event of an air attack on Freetown by Vichy French forces based in Dakar, Senegal. As the war progressed, members of the Sierra Leone Army were conscripted by the British War Office, while other civilians volunteered for service in the Royal Air Force.

My parents had been married for almost 10 years before I was born. This must have been a long anxious wait for both, especially in a society that valued children. My mother's inability to conceive must have been the subject of much talk, some sympathetic, some derisive, among friends and relatives. My parents were on the verge of adoption when I came along. The news of her pregnancy must have been received with great joy. But this joy was almost short lived as she nearly lost the pregnancy due to her predilection for Victorian health practises. She had taken castor oil to move her bowels which caused her much discomfort. But fate had decided otherwise, and the pregnancy went full term. I was born at Dr. Radcliff Jones' Nursing Home, at 7 Walpole Street, at 5:00am. The news of my birth and sex was delivered to my Uncle Dodd, who was staying with my family at 29 Pultney Street, Freetown. He had the privilege of announcing my birth to my father. The story goes that my father, in great excitement, put on his clothes as he descended the stairs to make his way to the nursing home, which was within easy walking distance.

I was christened Sylvester Modupe Broderick Jr., named after my father who had changed his middle name from "Boston" to "Modupe" when he was a student in America in the 1920s. I would later change "Sylvester" to "Sundiata" when I was a student in America in the 1960s. My mother informed me that my one-year birthday party was well attended by relatives, friends and their children; and that Donald Smythe-Macaulay, whose parents were family friends, had the honour of giving my birthday speech, an observation confirmed years later by Donald, himself when we met in the United States. My god brother, Henry Maduka Steady, who lived on Soldier Street, close to our house, must have been at the party as well as his father and my father were the best of friends. Maduka must have been three years old when I turned one, and probably has no recollection of the event. Maduka was my father's god son and Maduka's father would later be my sister's godfather. My godfather was Uncle Dodd, and my godmothers were Mrs. Sarah Luke, spouse of Justice Emile Luke and a dear friend of my mother, and Miss Carrie Hargrave, an African-American missionary who had been in Sierra Leone in the late thirties and early forties, serving as principal of the Reuben Johnson Memorial School.[12] I later met her in the late sixties in Wilmington, North Carolina when I lived in

---

[12] . According to my mother-in-law, the Reverend Muriel Alice Fitzjohn, she remembers the school and thinks it was located on Bathurst Street in Freetown, although she is not a hundred percent sure. The school must have ceased functioning in the forties, as I do not recall it in the fifties.

Greensboro, where I taught French at the North Carolina Agricultural and Technical State University.

My recollections of 29 Pultney Street, located in the centre of town, are scanty as we moved to Brookfields in 1944, the year of my sister's birth (Ore Emma Broderick). I was three. I do have vague memories of sitting on my father's lap on the veranda overlooking the street with a view of the famous Cotton Tree and Law Courts building, watching people and cars go by. My mother told me that I became intrigued by the sound of a steamroller that went up and down the road. Each time it went by I would mimic the sound of the engine by saying rhythmically, "ding, ding, ding." My parents imitating me when they saw a steamroller would utter the sound that I made. Consequently, I thought that the name of a steamroller was "ding, ding, ding." One day in infant school, I was surprised when the teacher told me that was not the name. I was also surprised when I discovered from a cousin that the expression "mo,mo,mo," which I used with my parents and they with me for going to the toilet, was not the correct term. Indeed, my cousin had laughed at me when I used the expression - what can one expect from a four-year old! When my nephews and niece were growing up, Mama would baby talk with them by saying ding, ding, ding. They later called her Grandma Dings. I had to tell them how that name came about. I also recall the steps that led to the third floor, a cat of which I was fond of, and partaking in the cat's meal, together with the cat, for which my mother scolded me. Mama told me a story of how my father would hold me on his lap in one hand and use the other to tune his short-wave radio (self-radio as it was known in Sierra Leone) with the other. A short-wave radio was a major source for receiving news about the war and other international news and could be found in many middle - class homes. When I was about two, (terrible twos) I would climb the chair on which my father sat, reach for the radio, and start turning the tuning knob. I did this frequently and ended up dislocating the tuning knob's calibration. My strong interest in gadgets had started that early, a trait that I inherited from my mother and passed on to my daughter.

Chapter: 5

Me at Five Years - Exploring My neighbourhood, Being Mischievous, Discovering Relatives and Making Friends

World War Two was still in full swing when we moved to Brookfields in 1944, the year of the Allied Invasion of Normandy. The area was locally known as "Grassfield" then because of its semi-rural landscape. I do not recall anything about this major war event, which must have produced much talk in Freetown's colonial society. However, I do recall there was a piece of land that stretched from the area that became Hannah Benka-Coker Street to lower King Harman Road, on which barracks had been built for housing soldiers. I remembered army trucks laden with singing soldiers moving in and out of the compound. One section of this stretch of land, bordering on King Harman Road, --where President Siaka Stevens's home is currently located—was littered with automobile and machine parts, and I enjoyed walking around the area with my father to collect some of these machine parts, which I played with. When the war ended a year later, the barracks were eventually dismantled. The stretch of land became the location for building the Freetown Secondary School for Girls and the government owned Youyi Building, which housed a few ministries. A portion of the area also became a field for playing football/soccer. We moved to number 14 King Harman Road in Brookfields, a two-story house with a cellar and a big yard full of fruit trees, mostly mangoes of various species: (Cherry, common, rope-rope, as they are known in Krio, the local language of the Krio people and lingua franca of Sierra Leone). There were also other fruit trees such as dita, orange, lokos, lemon grass, eucalyptus, and a tree whose bark could be used as an eraser. This was an idyllic setting for me. I became good at climbing the trees and relished picking the ripe mangoes. At the southern perimeter of the yard was a small stream with fish in it. I was intrigued by the fish and would go to the stream just about every day to watch them move around. Great was my disappointment one day when the fish went away due to the stream being blocked by roadwork. It was a big loss for me. I thought they would come back some day, but they never did. There was also land on which my mother planted vegetables and other food items: pepper, tomatoes, lettuce, cassava, potatoes, bananas, corn, etc. There was also a football field (Richmond Grounds as it was known) where the Methodist Boys High School (a secondary school) would hold their inter-house games and other sporting activities and on which I played with children in the neighbourhood. The whole complex, (house, yard, and football/soccer field) belonged to the Methodist Mission, the patrons from which my father rented the property. External to the house were spacious fields stretching up to Merewether Road (now Jomo Kenyatta Road) with hills in the background. Later the colonial government, built bungalows for their British colonial officers in this area of Brookfields, which stretched to Congo Valley. During the rainy season, there would be streams of water flowing down the fields from the hills that found their way into the Congo River. That's probably why the area was named "Brookfields."

One day while playing with my baby sister in the living room area of the house, I started to chase her and lost control of my speed and crashed into the edge of a table which produced a nasty gash over my left eye just above the eyebrow. My father, who watched us play, immediately drove me to the main hospital in Freetown (Connaught) where a stitch was placed over the cut. I still bear the mark of this stitch and gash to this day. When my mother found out about the incident, she was not pleased with my father as she felt he had been negligent in his oversight. When we got ill, my parents took my sister and me to see Dr. Radcliff Jones' at his nursing home where both of us had been born.

Following the death of Dr. Radcliff Jones in 1950, we benefited from the services of a famous retired druggist with the Health Department, Mr. Kingston King, who lived about a mile and a half from our house in the heart of Brookfields. His clinic served tons of people and their children in the neighbourhood. It was the first source for primary health care in the neighbourhood.

My interest in cars and being able to use my hands to do things or just being mischievous started around this time. One day there were some mechanics working on my father's car and I watched them pour a liquid into the gasoline tank. While their attention was focused on other things, I took a bottle of water and poured it into the tank. I probably had seen my father pour water into the radiator and thought I could do the same with the gasoline tank. I did not know that liquids for the car (oil, gasoline, and water) had special openings for their entry into the car's engine. Of course, the car would not start, and the mechanics and my father were becoming irritated. Noticing their frustration, I quickly went to my mother and nervously told her what I had done. She immediately informed my father of the mishap. The tank had to be emptied and refilled with untainted gasoline. I do not remember getting a spanking for my naughtiness, but my actions around the car were henceforth closely monitored.

On another occasion Papa brought home for my sister and me a tricycle with a carriage. It was a gift from a relative in Fernando Po (Bioko) - Uncle Wilfred, we called him, although I did not know how he was related to my mother, my maternal parent with the Fernando Po connection. I immediately jumped on the tricycle and started pedalling away on the lower veranda of the house. I pedalled fast without realising that I was coming to the end of the pavement and there was a slight drop. Not knowing how to bring the tricycle to a stop, I went over the drop and broke the wooden portion which connected the carriage to the tricycle frame. Luckily, I was not hurt but the tricycle was non-functional. The accident happened within 20 minutes of my father's arrival. I got a scolding from him for being careless. He later had the tricycle repaired and I was back to riding within a month. I very much enjoyed riding the tricycle with my sister in the carriage. But as we grew older, the board would give way, which necessitated several more repairs. Finally, the tricycle gave up for good.

Neighbourhood friends from the era were Bankole Saunders and his siblings, Remi, and Shola. Banky, as he was fondly known, would later become a fast bowler on the St Edwards School Cricket Team in the 1950s. An older friend was Prince, Olu, Williams, son of nurse Horton's sister and his cousin, Abigail (daughter of Nurse Horton, later Davies). In the early 50s when we had moved to Main Motor Road, Prince had a bicycle which he would let me ride at the Recreation Grounds. Further afield, up Riverside Drive, were another set of friends that I played with. They were the Terrys, Eugene, his twin sisters, (Joyce and Joya), Ariola and Otto, the Frazers (Henry and Donald) and relatives of the Beoku Betts who lived in Congo Valley (Mark Muehlemann, Gervais Beoku-Betts, and James Massalay. There were other young people in this household, but they were much older than us. Mrs. Taiwo Nelson, became my parents' helper and her children Edward, Simeon, Herbert, and Rosaline would visit frequently. Another member of the household was Iye Gorvie, a foster child. She and my sister would play together. She stayed with us until 1953 when she re-joined her parents in Bo.

My cousin, Dennis Lewis, used to spend weekends with us. He was like a big brother as he was six years my senior. He taught me how to play football/soccer, helped me with my homework and explored my neighbourhood with me. Dennis's mother, Aunty Queenie Lewis, was my father's younger sister, and she and her family (husband Uncle Sammy, Cousin Tunde, Cousin Ebun, Cousin Femi, and Regina), lived at the Broderick family house on 6 Circular Road. This was our home away from home. At an early age, I remember my sister and I going to Aunty Queenie's house three times a week after school (Monday,

Wednesday, and Friday) where we played, ate, and my sister would have her hair braided by my cousin Ebun. There was a mango tree in the yard which I enjoyed climbing. My aunt would plead with me to come down the tree, as she was very much concerned about my safety. My father would pick us up in the evenings to take us back to 14 King Harman Road. Those visits were precious as my cousin Dennis would take me to the Old Burial Ground playing field (Queen Elizabeth Playing Field/Sewa Grounds, next to Victoria Park) where he paid three pence to have me taught how to ride a bicycle. Through him, I met a different crowd of boys who were all older than me. His older siblings were protective of me and made sure that their younger brother was taking good care of me. Regina, the youngest cousin, was closer in age to me. She was three years my senior. She would take me to the market and other places when she went on errands. Today she is the only surviving family member of that generation from number 6th Circular Road. Regina lives in London with her husband, Harold Mason. The family property at 6 Circular Road was completely burnt to the ground during the rebel invasion of Freetown in January 2000.

Another relative who visited with us during the late forties was Cousin Asie, Florence Peters (now Mrs. Mahoney), from the Gambia, daughter of my father's first cousin, Mrs. Kezia Peters (nee Broderick). Cousin Asie came to Freetown to catch a ship to go to the UK to further her studies. She would later complete her studies in History from the School of Oriental and African Studies of the University of London. I'm told she was the Gambia's first Ph.D. I remember her being chatty and friendly. Her younger brother, Lenrie Peters, was in Freetown to attend sixth form at the Prince of Wales Secondary School in the late forties. He completed his medical studies at Cambridge University and returned to the Gambia to start a successful medical practice. He would become one of Africa's leading writers in the 1960s and 1970s.

In 2000, while my family and I lived in Conakry, we visited with my Gambian cousins in Banjul.

While at 14 King Harman Road, Papa had started building the family house on Main Motor Road, later Rasmusson Street, which was within easy walking distance from our current abode. To ease the building expenses, he had the cement bricks made in the yard. I used to watch the masons mix the cement with sand and water and put the mortar into the brick-making machine and then bring down the handle to pound the mortar into a brick. They would take the brick and set it down in an open space, exposed to the elements. The masons told me that the rain was good for making the bricks firm. Periodically, they transported the bricks to the site at 3 Main Motor Road.

Chapter: 6

Formal Education in Sierra Leone From Kindergarten to Secondary School

Kindergarten: Saint Anne and Buxton Infants

I started infants/kindergarten in 1945 at the St Joseph's Convent (Saint Anne) on Howe Street, which makes me an old boy of a girls' school. I recall the names of three students from that era: Willy Short, Suzanette Stanley and Colvin Nicol, all three now deceased. Later, when we moved to Rasmusson Street in 1950, Suzanette and her family lived on that street. As children, I played with her brothers (Freddy, Joseph, and Teddy) at the Recreation Grounds or on the tennis courts behind my family's house. I used to enjoy having her around as I had a crush on her. Willy Short and his family eventually moved to Ghana, and we lost touch with each other.

Catechism was strongly emphasised at the school, and I recall being told who God was and that he was everywhere, including the playing ground which I could see from the classroom. The omnipresence of God was not an easy concept for a four-year old to comprehend. I remember asking whether he was in the classroom while being outside on the playground, to which the teacher said, "Yes." I retorted that I could not see him. "He is a spirit and that is why you cannot see him. But he is everywhere," she concluded.

In January 1947, I started Buxton Infants School at Charles Street. I discovered that discipline was more strongly enforced than had been my experience at Saint Joseph's Convent. We had to form lines to march to our classes every day, except when it rained. I was lucky to have been selected to play in the school band whose music accompanied the march. I very much enjoyed being a member of the band. A student of the day with whom I became friends was Lewis Tanimola Pratt. He was also a member of the band, and we played our respective instruments together. There were other students with whom I became friends whose names I have, unfortunately, forgotten. Nevertheless, I do recall teachers such as Miss Decker and Miss Parkinson and the Head Mistress, Miss Williams, who was very strict. Miss Williams and her family were very religious and as a result were commonly referred to as "Holy Williams." I recall an incident when she detained me after school. Papa came to pick me up and was told that I had been naughty. As she did not let me go with him, when he exited her office, I thought he had gone and left without me. I became very worried. Fifteen minutes later, which seemed an eternity, she let me go. I hastily dashed away believing my father had left me behind only to find him sitting in his car patiently waiting for me. I was so happy to see him.

In November of 1948, the British Broadcasting Corporation (BBC) reported that Princess Elizabeth, the heir to the British throne, had given birth to a bouncing baby boy who would be later named Prince Charles, a future King of Great Britain and the British Common- wealth of Nations. The news must have been reported in the Sierra Leone Daily Mail, the principal newspaper of the day and was the talk of town among members of the colonial government. When the students arrived at school that morning, Miss Williams asked them if they knew what had happened in the United Kingdom. Both Lewis (Tani) Pratt and I raised our hands. She pointed to Lewis who confirmed the birth of Prince Charles.

On days when Papa did not pick me up from school, Miss Williams and I would walk to Papa's office at the Secretariat Building, a huge building in the centre of Freetown, which was close to her house on George Street. Obviously, this had been pre-arranged. She would drop me off at his office where he would be waiting for me. One day when she dropped me off, Papa was not there, so I waited for him. I waited and waited and waited but he did not show up. Apparently, he must have forgotten me, I concluded. So, I decided I was going to walk home to Brookfields. First, I considered going to my aunt's house at No. 6 Circular Road (which was a shorter distance compared to my parent's house on King Harman Road in Brookfields), but then decided against it. So, I walked from George Street to Westmoreland Street (now Siaka Stevens Street), to Sanders Street, to Savage Street, and then to King Harman Road. My mother could not believe her eyes when she saw me. I assured her that I had been very careful all the way. I don't remember what Papa said to me when he came home for the panic that I caused. I knew I did not get a spanking. They were all too happy to see me. I must have been six going on seven when this incident occurred. Ever since that event Papa was always timely in picking me up from school until I was old and responsible enough to walk home by myself.

At Buxton School, I participated in the school's choir and took part in the annual singing competition held at the British Council. I dare say that I had a good voice, and I continued singing in the choir at the Model School, Prince of Wales and later in the Otterbein University Men's Glee Club when I was a student in America. Papa had wanted me to sing with the choir at Saint George's Cathedral. I joined the choir in 1951 on a probationary status and attended choir practises twice a week. When Papa found out that we young boys spent a good part of our time at choir practice playing football in the street behind the Big Market building, he stopped me from going to choir practice. Much to my disappointment, I never sang in the Cathedral choir, as did my other friends.

My first use of a telephone took place in my father's office at the Secretariat Building. His office was on the third floor so we would take the lift/elevator up, operated by a conductor whom I envied because I thought he had a great job riding the elevator all day long. I was eager to use a phone, so my father called his friend the Reverend Dr. Steady and I had the opportunity to speak with my godbrother, Maduka Steady. This was in 1947. I have referred to a telephone in Freetown only to demonstrate the availability of this item in the country as early as 1947. I'm not sure of its year of introduction in Sierra Leone. But it may have been introduced in the 1930s. Mentioning of the telephone and the elevator serve as a metaphor to underscore the functioning of the services provided during the colonial times and which lasted until the early seventies.

Primary Training at the Government Model School

In January 1949, I transferred from Buxton School to the Government Model School located at the intersection of Berry Street and Circular Road. It was then a single-story primary school as opposed to its status of being a secondary school with two stories. This is where I commenced my primary schooling. It was a much larger school with classes from Standard One to Standard Six. The headmaster of the school was Mr. H. Knox-Macaulay. Later, he took up an appointment with the Education Department and was replaced by a Mr. Morgan. Lewis Pratt, my classmate at the Buxton Infants School, had also transferred to the Model School, and he and I were in standard one. I soon made friends with other classmates such as Dalton Macaulay, Donald Frazer, Morley Wright, Naib Iscandari, Nicholas (Nick) Palmer, Philip Gage, Richard Gordon Harris, Alfred Sawyer, Mohammed Mahdi, Crispin Cross, Cyril Macaulay, Godson Leopold, Richard During, and others. By popular opinion the pretty girls were Doreen Macaulay, Fredericka John, and Evelyn Peters. There were other pretty girls, but they were not in our class. The day started with an assembly attended by students and teachers, followed by biblical readings, singing of hymns, and culminating with the Lord's Prayer. The headmaster would then give his address, and, at its conclusion, dismiss us to our classrooms. Our teacher was Miss Williams. When we moved to Standard Two, our teacher was again Miss Williams. In Standard Three we had Miss John and in Standard Four A, it was Miss Ursula Johnson, a very tall fair-skin woman. Mrs. Elliott was the teacher for standard Four B. I recall Miss John and Miss Johnson being very strict teachers.[13] Some students joined the group in standard two and three. There were other teachers who were well known. These included Mr. Campbell who was feared because he liked to use the cane. He later got into trouble for other reasons than using the cane and was sanctioned for malfeasance. There was also Mr. Vincent whom we affectionately called "Vinco." He was also very strict but had a broad welcoming smile. Finally, was Mr. Fewry who conducted lessons for students at his residence after school. I became a cub scout. Other cub scouts included Dalton Macaulay, Lewis Pratt, Nicholas Palmer, Morley Wright, Alfred Sawyer, Donald Frazer, Naib Iscandari, etc. Our cub mistress was Miss Jarrett. We had our cub scout meetings on Thursday afternoons at the school grounds. The school's scoutmaster was Mr. Gorvie.

One of the big school events was the Empire Day Celebration that took place at the Recreation Grounds in Brookfields, now the home of Siaka Stevens Stadium. Prior to the march past there was a sports competition, track, and field events, involving both primary and secondary schools; and on the day of the march past, schools would march to receive their trophies and salute the Governor. On such occasions, we scouts, and cubs led the school during the march past. The position order of the march was based on the date a school was founded. Model School was opened in 1912 and so it was probably one of the lead primary schools to march into the Recreation Grounds. Once the trophies had been distributed and the salute taken by the Governor, we would march to exit the grounds accompanied by the music of Sierra Leone Military

---

[13]. Appended is an incomplete list of students of the era from Standard One through standard four, 1949-52)

Battalion or the Police Force. This would be the moment when the marching got intense. Buoyed up by the music, the cheers, and shouts of the crowd, students would engage in showing off their fancy footwork or displaying their strutting skills. Outside the grounds we would march back to the school grounds to be dismissed, our trophies proudly on display. On other occasions we participated in the Scout Jamboree Celebrations at the Prince of Wales School grounds. We cubs and scouts marched from the Old Burial Ground/Queen Elizabeth II Playing Field/Sewa Grounds) to the Prince of Wales School and back. At the Prince of Wales scouts would display their scouting skills and listen to an address by the Governor or Chief Scout. A Model School Scout, who later became a neighbour and good friend, was John Edward Bankole Jones. He and his family moved to Brookfields (Lower King Harman Road) in 1955. John would later become the godfather of my son Ahovi Broderick.

Going home from school was a bonding activity. It was an occasion for teasing one another, telling stories, speculating on the future, commenting on happenings at the school, discussing teachers, girlfriends, whom we referred to as "wives", sports, and current events. During my first year, my father continued to take me to school and had someone from home pick me up after school. We would walk home from Circular Road to No. 14 King Harman Road. The following year, I was judged old enough to walk home by myself. I used to walk home with friends from the Brookfields area—the Sawyers (Colin and Alfred) and the Frazers (Henry and Donald). We would walk from Circular Road to Pademba Road to Merewether Road (now Jomo Kenyatta Road) where the Sawyers would drop off at New England Ville, and the Frazers and I would continue to Admiralty Road, where they dropped off, and I would continue alone down King Harman Road to number 14. On Merewether Road were homes with lovely gardens inhabited by colonial British officials. We admired these gardens, which were very well maintained. One day as we walked home, we decided to uproot some of the flowers for planting in our respective home gardens. Following a hasty look, we concluded there was no one around observing us. So, we uprooted a few flowers and off we went. No sooner had we done this than a gardener appeared, and he started to pursue us. We took to our heels. Eventually, he gave up, and we thought the incident was over. So, we continued with our walk, merrily chatting away. A few minutes later I happened to turn around and there was the gardener in hot pursuit of us again. I sounded the alarm and off we went, this time running all the way to the intersection of Admiralty Road and King Harman Road, thereby outdistancing the gardener. By the time we got to the intersection, the gardener was no longer in sight, he had given up the pursuit, and we all gave a sigh of relief but kept a watchful eye to make sure he did not try to outsmart us again. The Frazers continued home on Admiralty Road to Cantonment Road, and I went down King Herman Road to Number 14. In the weeks ahead, following this incident, we were very fearful of the gardener as we walked home on Merewether Road, but, happily for us, nothing ever did happen.

The route that took us to Pademba and Merewether Roads was, however, not the shortest way home for me, especially after my parents moved to 3 Main Motor Road in July 1950. Accordingly, I joined another walking-home group comprising students who lived on Circular Road, Campbell Street, and Saint John. In this group were such students as Dalton Macaulay, (who had a short way to go as he lived on Circular Road, not far from the school) Nicholas (Nick) Palmer, Rotimi Paris, Bunting Bowen-Wright, Willy Grosvenor and me. There were girls who lived in the area, but we were not interested in having them being a part of a boy's group. We had several options of going home. Sometimes we went up the greens to Tower Hill, where we had a beautiful view of Freetown, and then descended to Circular Road. Sometimes we went through the Quarry at the Public Works Department. Sometimes we went through West Street to Dundas Street and then to Campbell Street to

Saint John. Sometimes we went down Mends Street to Campbell Street. In all these options, I was the last to get home. The last drop-off point on this route was Saint John where Nick, Rotimi, Bunting, and Willy dropped off, and I would walk by myself, a mile further, down Savage Street to 3 Main Motor Road.

A major news item of the era was the death of His Majesty, King George the sixth, the King of Great Britain and the British Commonwealth of Nations, who had died in February of 1952. Nick, Bunting and I were going home that day. Willy had preceded us. When we got to Saint John, we ran into Willy who greeted us with the unlikely news of the King's death. Of course, we did not believe him and dismissed the news as being preposterous, and that Willy was up to his old tricks again. So, we parted company not believing a word. When I got home, I was greeted with the same news. My mother told me that the BBC had announced that the King had died in his sleep. I realised that Willy had told us the truth. We owed him an apology, I thought, but he never got one. Those of us who were scouts or cub scouts had to wear a black armband as a sign of mourning. I think we wore the band for three months.

I also recall a dump of disposed electronic materials on the roadside going up Tower Hill, and Bunting became interested in an item that he took home. Somehow, he got the item to function. I mention this incident to underscore Bunting's early interest in electronics. Today, he is the proud owner of Wright Electronics at his home on Campbell Street. He was also the fastest runner among us. His athletic skills made him feature prominently on the Sierra Leone Grammar's School track team.

An event that made Nick the butt of many jokes had to do with his father, "Bombas Palmer" as he was popularly known. Rumour had it that his father, a successful druggist and a feisty businessman, was known for giving "bombastic speeches." That was how he had earned the nickname "Bombas Palmer." It was common news in 1952 that Mr. Palmer took the Governor of Sierra Leone, Sir Beresford

Stokes, to court for reasons that we primary school students did not fully understand. The event produced much talk in Freetown. Here was a Sierra Leonean having the temerity of taking the King of England's representative to court. There was both admiration and remorse for Mr. Palmer's action. Some Sierra Leoneans considered his action justified and sympathised with his cause while others thought it irresponsible and were not in support. Nick enjoyed talking about his father, and on occasions would imitate his father giving a speech at the City Council where he was a counsellor. He would use words which we did not understand, neither did we know whether the words were English or not, but they sounded bombastic, and this produced much laughter among us. When he would stop, some of us prodded him to continue; and he would respond by giving more speeches, which in turn produced more laughter. Nick and I became life-long, good friends.

Another going-home activity had to do with football matches at the Parade Grounds on Tower Hill. Model School had a good football team composed of players such as Maxwell Peters and Ekundayo Iscandari. Maxwell was short and stocky and had bowlegs. He was also fast. He could do wonders with the ball, enabling him to dribble past his opponents and score goals. Ekundayo Iscandari was a great goalkeeper. He had skilful hands which enabled him to snatch the ball in the air. We used to say in Krio (I de bohkul di bohl) (he "snatches' ' the ball). Because of our good team, we easily defeated opponents such as Cathedral School, Ebenezer School, Buxton School, and Samaria School, whose teams were weaker when compared to Model School's team. We played in the western division and one of the big matches of the year was a game pitted against a team comprising the best players from the schools in the east and a team comprising the best players of schools from the west. The West won most of the games. Model School's strongest opponent was Saint Anthony, which always gave us a good game, but we won most of the encounters. Our exceptional performance made us feel invincible, boasting that our team could even defeat a Secondary School Team if put to the test. But this never happened.

A famous player on Saint Anthony's team was a boy whose nickname was "Size Ten." I do not recall his real name. He was nicknamed "Size Ten" because of his mammoth feet. One day I had the good fortune to walk with him accompanied by other boys; and as we walked and talked, I took the opportunity to observe his girth and bare feet, covered with red dust from the playing ground. They were indeed massive in the eyes of a nine-year old. His gigantic feet no doubt enabled him to blast very powerful shots that goalkeepers dared not defend. In kindergarten some of us wore shoes to school. However, most students went to primary school barefooted. We did not start to wear sandals to school until we were in Form Three in a Secondary School, but we wore shoes on special occasions: e.g., church-going and other social events.

At the Parade Grounds was a temperamental ex-soldier nicknamed "Morocco" who served as the custodian of the grounds. It was alleged that he was from Ghana and had served in the Second World War and probably taken part in the Allied Invasion of North Africa and may have been taken prisoner in Morocco. How he got to Sierra Leone I do not know, but he must have talked a lot about his experiences in Morocco and probably that was how he acquired the nickname "Morocco." He was an unpredictable character, possibly not altogether in the head. There were occasions when he forbade a game for no apparent reason and had to be cajoled. The word would spread that Morocco said, "No Game," to which we would respond in unison, "No Game." Indeed, there was no game. However, a few shillings did the trick, and Morocco would let the game proceed.

In 1951, I changed my home-going routine. My parents instructed me to pick up my sister from the Holy Trinity Infants School, which she attended. The school was located on the East side of Freetown, and we lived in the West. I had to walk down Circular Road in the opposite direction towards Regent Road to Goderich Street and then to the school at the bottom of Kissy Road where I collected my sister from Miss Carrie Thomas, (fondly named Teacher Carrie) the Head Mistress, and then caught the double-decker bus at the Annie Walsh School Bus Stop for a long ride to Brookfields. I did this until my sister transferred to Cathedral School the following year, which was in the centre of town and closer to home. A major event of that year was the introduction of Double Decker Buses to Freetown by the Government of Sierra Leone Road Transport Department. School children had just returned to the Water Street train station from a New Year's Day outing at Courban's farm in Songo. As the train pulled into the station that evening, half a dozen newly-arrived double decker buses, splendidly lit, descended Wilberforce Street, and made the turn into Water Street (now Wallace Johnson Street) and then to Rawdon Street and then to Oxford Street (now Lightfoot Boston Street) where they were parked at the Oxford Street station, in front of the Bank of British West Africa, as it was known then. The school children cheered lustily as the buses went by. Later that year, a famous Sierra Leonean singer composed the song "Welcome to Sierra Leone double decker buses" which became a popular hit. The double decker buses transported passengers from Cline Town on the East side of Freetown to Congo Cross station on the West. There were also single decker buses that transported passengers to other areas of Freetown on a regular basis. In the morning and evenings, there were single decker buses that transported passengers to and from the Mountain Villages (Wilberforce, Regent, Bathurst, and Charlotte) and Sea-Side villages (Lumley, Aberdeen, Murray Town, Goderich, Hamilton, Sussex, York and Kent, Wellington, Hastings, and Waterloo). There were also vouchers on sale at an office close to the Train Station, which students could buy and surrender as payment to the bus conductor for a bus ride.

In 1952 a story that gripped Freetown was the Janet

Bundle Scare. It was alleged that a woman by the name of Janet carried a big bundle into which she placed children whom she had captured. She was a spirit, popularly referred to as wonsho[14] in Krio. It was unsafe to be out in the streets after 9:00pm as a child would likely fall prey to her. I remember attending a concert at the Cathedral School that ended after 9:30pm and being very scared to walk home to Brookfields with friends. However, with time the scare diminished, and life returned to normal.

Secondary Training at the Prince of Wales School:

I entered the Prince of Wales (POW) School in January 1953, having passed the Common Entrance Examination the previous year. It was the year of Queen Elizabeth's the second's coronation and the conquest of Mount Everest by Edmund Hillary and Tenzing Norgay. These events triggered a lot of British-led activities in Freetown which required the participation of Secondary Schools. I was admitted to the preparatory class. A few of my classmates from Model School were also admitted to the Prince of Wales that year and were in the same class. Among them were Nicholas Palmer, Naib Iscandari, Richard Gordon Harris (Nqobisizwe Akintunde Adekayode), Philip Gage, Crispin Cross (who went to Form One). Others such as Dalton Macaulay, Morley Wright, Bunting Bowen-Wright went to the Sierra Leone Grammar School. I dare say that three fourths of the class had passed the Common Entrance Examination which gave access to secondary schooling. The bulk of the boys from our Model School class had gone to these two schools (the Prince of Wales and Grammar Schools, the latter being the oldest and famous secondary school in West Africa having been founded in 1845 by the Church Missionary Society.) A few went to the Methodist Boys High School and to the Albert Academy. As for the

---

[14]. A spirit that moved with great speed, like a breeze it was often said.

girls, it must have been a split between the Annie Walsh Memorial School and the Methodist Girls High School. Lewis Pratt had preceded us to the Prince of Wales the previous year following his return from the United Kingdom where he had gone to school while his parents were living there. Upon his return to Freetown, he went straight to the Prince of Wales.

My godbrother, Maduka Steady, had also gone to the Prince of Wales. It was reassuring to find him there. Attending secondary schools, located in different areas of the city, negatively impacted the Model School group's cohesion. For example, contacts among those of us who had gone to a different secondary school, as opposed to the same school, became far and few between. Accordingly, we lost touch with one another on a weekly basis. Occasionally, we met at football games or at inter-school events. But as time passed, old friendships waned as new friendships were formed.

The first day of the new school year at the Prince of Wales is joyful and fearful, joyful because newcomers are proud to be in a secondary school donned in their new uniforms and frightful because of hazing traditions that await them. Our form master, Mr. Adams, was in the classroom and his presence made us feel protected, as we surmised that our adversaries, mainly students in forms 2 and 3, would not dare enter the classroom to haze us. Unfortunately, this assurance was short-lived. Much to our disappointment, he left the room as the time for recess approached. Consequently, we were alone--lame ducks waiting to be preyed upon. To avert the impending pandemonium, we decided to lock the door. But unfortunately for us, our classroom was sandwiched between two classes (Forms 2A and 2B) and there was a large hole in the wall between our class and Form 2B. So, we barricaded the hole with desks and chairs. No sooner had we done this than the bell sounded for recess. The older boys descended upon us with gleam in their eyes--like vultures attacking their prey. They tried to enter through the main door and found it locked. This made them furious. Then someone among them said, "let's go through the hole that leads from our classroom into theirs." They found the hole blocked. They became more annoyed. Being older and stronger than us, more in control of the situation, they eventually overpowered our poor defence and entered our classroom. They unlocked the door, and more of them entered. We were now at their mercy. We were taunted, insulted, and slapped, and the fact that we had the impudence to put up a defence made the experience worse. That day I went home with a headache. As our adversaries departed the room, they "consoled" us with the assurance that next year would be our turn to do the same to newcomers. The next day those boys who had not been present for the first day of school were hazed. However, a handful of newcomers did not attend school until the third or fourth day. I do not know the reason that informed their decision, but it turned out to be wise. By the third and fourth day the zeal to haze the other newcomers had died; and so, these latecomers went unscathed.

The Prince of Wales is a government-operated school founded by His Royal Highness the Prince of Wales (later Edward the VIII) during a visit to Freetown in 1925. Being a government school, it had resources and privileges not provided at other secondary schools. For example, all books (text and exercise) were supplied free of charge, which was not the case in other secondary schools where students had to purchase their text and exercise books. Students in Prep, Form One and Two were provided free food during the lunch period. The food was known as "condor." (Rice cooked in large quantities as for schools, colleges, and prisons, etc.[15]) There were also women who sold local foods. One of them was a Mrs. Dundas who was renowned for her akara cakes (banana fritters). The school

---

[15]. Clifford N. Fyle and Eldred D. Jones, *A Krio-English Dictionary*, P. 189, Oxford University Press and Sierra Leone University Press, 1980.

fees, per term, may have been less than what the other secondary schools required. The school was noted for its science classes and had produced several famous doctors and engineers and civil servants during its short life span (twenty-three years by the time I entered.) Examples included the Honourable Sanusi Mustapha (Minister of Finance), Dr. Raymond Easmon (renowned physician), Dr. Davidson Nicol, one of Sierra Leone's erudite/illustrious scholars; also accomplished in Medical Sciences –became Principal of the University of Sierra Leone, and a successful international civil servant, having obtained university degrees in both the Sciences and the Arts; and, Mr. Wadi Williams, (first class engineer). The school also had several Sierra Leonean and British teachers with first degrees and advanced teachers' certificates. The year of my entry, Mr. Constance Tuboku-Metzger, a former physics teacher, who was trained in the United States, had become the first Sierra Leonean to be principal of the school. We had several teachers who were specialists in English (Language and Literature), English History, Mathematics, Latin, French, Science (Biology, Chemistry and Physics), Geography, Art, and Woodwork. I was good at Geography, History and English and Woodwork and later developed a penchant for science. I joined the school's choir under the direction of Professor D. C. Parker who took the school's choir to several singing competitions where we featured prominently. We also performed on Speech Day during which we led the school in singing the School Song, ("Come swell the chorus, one and all, and join the ranks with me".) I was a member of the choir during my entire tenure at the school. Of treasured memory, besides the School Song, were three songs that Professor Parker introduced to the choir, Jupiter the Planets, "I Vow to thee my Country," Bach's "Jesu Joy of Man's Desiring," and Hugh S. Roberton, "All in the April Evening". Today, each time I hear these songs, my memory immediately goes back to those idyllic days of my first year at the Prince of Wales and to Professor Parker.

The Prince of Wales school is located by the edge of the sea, on the King Tom peninsular, an area on the western side of Freetown. A wall with a rusty gate separated the school from a jetty, which had been used during the Second World War. Swimming was a popular activity mainly done by students in Prep, Forms One, Two and Three. Older boys participated infrequently. My interest in swimming had started prior to my going to the Prince of Wales. My father was an avid swimmer, and he took me on Sunday mornings to Cockle Bay where he swam and taught me how to swim. During my first year at the Prince of Wales, it was a common occurrence for pupils to swim in the morning before classes started, during the midday recess break and after school. We swam in the nude, as we could not afford bathing suits. Some students who were good swimmers dared to swim across Kroo Bay and back, and others would swim to where the launch, Kingtom, was anchored and back. My friend Nick and I were swimming rivals. We always competed as to who was faster. Sometimes he won and sometimes I did. After a swim, boys would wash the salt off their bodies by going under a shower whose top was missing. Then we would allow our bodies to dry off as we had no towels, and then put on our clothes. The swimming was not supervised. It was a free for all activity. Unfortunately, a tragic incident happened in July 1953. The mayor's son, Kenneth Taylor-Cummings, drowned. I remember how I got the news of the drowning. It was a Saturday afternoon and Papa and I had attended a football game at the Football Association Grounds in Kingtom. After the game, instead of taking the road that passed in front of the school where we certainly would have seen crowds talking about the drowning, we took the other way that went around the Kingtom peninsular, thereby missing the scene.

Papa drove to the junction of Sanders Street and Upper Brook Street where he sent me to a store to get bread. While there, I overheard people talking casually about someone who had drowned and one person questioning the veracity of the incident. I got my bread, and returned to the car, not knowing the identity of the person that drowned. I did not say anything to Papa. That evening he went to the Dinner Club and found out about the drowning which he told me the next day as I had gone to bed when he returned home from the club. I told him about the incident of the previous evening at the store but had not said a word because I did not know the identity of the person.

The viewing of Kenneth's body took place at his parents' residence on Charlotte Street; funeral service was at Wesley Church and interment at the Kissy Road Cemetery, where Albert Tuboku-Metzger, Jabez Thompson and I, standing next to one another, watched the lowering of the coffin into the grave. Kenneth was laid to rest in a watery grave as water flowed underground down from the Fourah Bay College hills. It was the middle of the raining season, and the month of July was noted for its heavy downpours. A motor pump had to be used to extract the water from the grave. It was my first viewing of a corpse and my first attendance at a funeral.

Fishermen using dynamite to catch fish was a common practice. When the dynamite exploded, the walls of those classrooms close to the sea would vibrate and if the dynamite was thrown during the recess period or after school, the boys would scramble to retrieve the floating fish. The dynamite gave the fish an unpleasant taste, so I stopped taking it home. On occasions the police tried to arrest the fishermen but were never successful. Following the drowning incident, the principal banned us from swimming, although some students who lived in the Kingtom area used to swim clandestinely. Years later, on a visit to Freetown from Guinea in 2006, I visited the school and looked through the gate that we used to climb over. The jetty was no longer there, the area that we landed when we climbed over the fence was almost gone due to erosion from the sea and squatters had occupied the sea-area that bordered the playing field.

Another serious accident at the POW concerned a javelin that struck a student in the neck. That morning, during assembly, the games' master, Mr. Thompson, had warned students to be very careful when throwing the javelin because of its potential danger. Unfortunately, some boys had not heeded the games master's warnings. The victim was rushed to the Connaught Hospital where he was treated. Luckily for him, the wound had not been fatal. Athletically, I developed my cricket skills by becoming a fast bowler. I played on my house team (Granville) as well as on the school's team. In 1958, I was a member of the team that travelled to the then Protectorate where we played matches against Njala College and the Magburaka' Training College. We won both matches. Other members of the team included but not limited to the following: Abdulai Kargbo (Captain), Farrell Cuthbert, Alex Kamara, Jonathan Sawyer, Tunde Thompson, Frankwin Jones, Modupe Broderick, Yaya Wurie, and Theodore Pratt, games master. (The list is incomplete)

Two major activities that students looked forward to being were Speech Day and the annual Sports Day that pitted competition among the four houses: Granville, Macauley, Mansfield and Wilberforce, climaxed by the inter house relay which produced much excitement. For Speech Day the students would be elegantly dressed in white, the school's formal uniform to welcome patrons, parents, and well-wishers. A play would be performed, songs were performed by the school's choir, the principal would give his address, and students who had achieved academic excellence would be recognized. Another activity that was of importance was the Empire Day Celebration that pitted sport competition in field and track activities against secondary schools. The Prince of Wales featured prominently in this competition as it had older boys who were in the sixth form, which gave the school an advantage.

I cannot conclude my reminiscences of the Prince of Wales without talking about one of our colourful teachers. There were maybe four colourful teachers that I recall. Of course, there could have been more depending on one's own experiences: Pa[16] Alieu Spillsbury, popularly referred to as "Alpha", Pa Dyke Harding, popularly referred to as "Abdulai Power," Pa. Tom Deigh (popularly referred to as T. S. Novum) and Mr. C. R. A. Cole, known as "CRA-Cole." I had all four teachers and surely have stories to tell about each one of them, but I will focus on Mr. Spillsbury and a Latin teacher and a few others who will remain nameless. Mr. Spillsbury was known for being a strict disciplinarian in the school. He had the habit of peering over his glasses from his desk to address students. When he gave you that stare, you can be sure something was going to happen. One day he noticed that I was talking with another student, not paying attention to what he was saying. So, he called me out and made me stand at the side of the classroom. While he was explaining something on Geography on the blackboard, he noticed that I was not paying attention, so he threw the duster at me. I saw the throw in the nick of time and noticed that the trajectory of the throw was heading towards my legs. I was agile enough to spread my legs apart to prevent the duster from hitting me. The duster went between my legs and hit the wall. Then he quickly retorted, "I missed to score a goal." A burst of laughter engulfed the class. On another occasion, he commented that I was overfed and attributed my size to eating for two because my father, whom he knew very well, was away from Sierra Leone. That name stuck as my classmates called me "overfed." He called another student a "black beetle", because of his dark complexion and his penchant for talking. Teasing or name calling of students predicated on teachers' remarks was a common occurrence and no one was spared as it was a shared belief that someday it would be your turn; and you would receive the same level of teasing depending on the manner that you had dished it out. Corporal punishment was frequently used to enforce physical and or mental discipline. Mr. Spillsbury was fond

---

[16]. A term of high respect meaning "Father"

of saying to the culprit, "turn your waist to an angle of ninety degrees," and then administered the cane. We had a Latin teacher who would mete out this form of discipline for failing to decline a noun or conjugate a verb correctly. He would walk up and down an aisle asking questions. When a student failed to give the correct answer, that student was asked to stand on his chair and receive two strokes of the cane on his buttocks. Each time we had Latin it was a foregone conclusion that we were going to be caned. Fortunately for us, the Latin Class was the first of the afternoon session following the midday recess. During the break, we would go to the toilets and pad our derrieres with exercise books to diminish the sting of the caning that we were sure to receive. When the teacher hit the buttocks, the cane made a sound. Startled by the sound, the teacher remarked, "Boy, you must have the hide of a rhinoceros." And then he would administer the second stroke noting, "Boy, you don't feel" and the student quickly replied, "No Sir, I feel Sir, I feel Sir." The class giggled with laughter. The teacher never found out what was going on. Another teacher was more cunning in administering corporal punishment. The teacher would aim the cane to hit the culprit's fingertips, where it hurt the most, rather than the palm of the hand. To instil fear in us students, this teacher would say to the class, "when I beat, I bruise, I leave scars, I leave my trademark for generations yet unborn." Another teacher would admonish, "Boy I warn you. You come here empty, you go out empty, you smoke and you drink, no spark of home training whatsoever. You are worse than the Bay boys."

Today, this school, which used to be a model of a successful well-managed secondary school in Sierra Leone with the requisite results to show, has fallen on difficult times. The regression has required the old boys of the school as well as other secondary schools, of both genders, to play a pivotal role in their schools' upkeep. These former pupils are to be found not only in Sierra Leone and West Africa but also in countries in Europe and North America.

They have acquired skills that have made them highly marketable and are thus able to seek employment internationally as healthcare providers, educationists, lawyers, scientists, engineers, entrepreneurs etc., as the Sierra Leone Government does not have the capacity to absorb them.

Since achieving independence in April 1961, Sierra Leone has experienced a brutal civil war that lasted some 12 years, and which brought much mayhem and destruction to the nation. The economic and political regression has also resulted in an Ebola outbreak that killed over several thousand of Sierra Leoneans and devastated the health service system. In addition, the decline triggered a major landslide due to uncontrolled deforestation, bad governance and overpopulation. As the Government does not have the financial resources to support the upkeep of schools and the payment of teachers' salaries, it has become the responsibility of former pupils living abroad to raise funds in support of their secondary schools and families. For example, in the United Kingdom and the United States of America, there are several chapters of these secondary schools whose members provide annual financial support to their respective alma maters.

Chapter: 7

Life at 3, Main Motor Road Later at 17 Rasmusson Street.

In June of 1950, we moved to our new house, Brookland's Villa, at 3 Main Motor Road, Brookfields. It was a common practice in Sierra Leone for houses to be named. For example, there was "King Jimmy House," "Fanjay House," "Malamah House" "My Nest" to name but a few. In 1958, the street was renamed Rasmusson and our house was re-assigned the number 17. It was alleged that the choice of the street's name was to honour a Mr. Rasmusson, of Danish extraction, who had designed the first four houses built on the street. I had monitored the growth from the time the bricks were being made when we lived at 14 King Harman Road. It was a modern 4-bedroom house for its day with an indoor toilet and bath facilities and an outdoor kitchen connected by a walkway to the pantry located on the second floor. It was built on land that was spacious and the surrounding areas had lots of open spaces, trees, and shrubs. There were five houses on the street when we moved and ours became the sixth. The first four were known as the "Ashoyebi" [17] houses. In the first lived the Stanleys, the next was inhabited by Mrs. Dawson (nee Clinton), the third Mrs. Songo Davies and the fourth Mrs. Clayton Davies. Between the fourth and our house was Mr. Brandon, a retired police officer. The Terry family lived for a short period in one of those houses in 1950 before moving to Riverside Drive where I got to know them. My mother became close friends with Mrs. Dawson and we got to know the young people of the house. They included Kate Davies

---

[17]. A Krio word derived from Yoruba signifying similarity in design, e.g., dress of the same kind worn by women on special occasions.

who lives in New York City, her younger sisters Frances and Admire Davies, Alfred Bockry and Marion Clinton, a niece of Mrs. Dawson. Marion completed her college education in the United States and later moved to Tanzania with her husband, a Tanzanian. She has since relocated to the US to join her children following her husband's demise. Alfred Bockry and I became good friends. Indeed, I had met him a year before on the Richmond football field at King Harman Road, prior to our move to Main Motor Road, but I did not know where he lived. I was thus delighted when I discovered that we lived on the same street and only a few doors away from each other. He was a naturally gifted athlete who excelled in football, cricket, tennis and track. He would make his mark in cricket and was the first from our group to play for the national team of Sierra Leone. Today he lives in Maryland following a long stint in Liberia. The Stanley boys (Freddy and Joseph) were successful in the services. Freddy became a commissioned officer in the Sierra Leone Army following his military training at Sandhurst Military Academy in the UK. Joseph became Commissioner of the Sierra Leone Police Force, and Teddy was an Economist with USAID/Liberia. Michael Clinton and his older sister, Dundee, a nephew, and niece of Mrs. Dawson, vacationed at their aunt's residence during the long school holidays. Michael emigrated to Ghana and lived with his family in Accra, for many years as a successful lawyer until his demise in 2022; Dundee lives in Freetown with her husband.

Life at 3 Main Motor Road was eventful. As we had a big yard and a "spacious house" for its day I used to play with neighbourhood friends in our yard or on the bottom veranda or in the garage or on the front steps. One day a friend and I were playing on the bottom veranda. We were playing a game of heading the ball. The objective was to head the ball past your opponent to score a goal. If the ball dropped before it got to your opponent, you had the option of heading the ball from that spot. My friend headed the ball towards a window, and I made a dash to catch the ball and crashed into the glass window, slashing my left wrist. The blood gushed out. Out of fright, my play friend took to his heels. I had to call Mrs. Nelson who rushed to help me. Fortunately for me my father arrived in his car a few minutes later. He immediately took me to Connaught Hospital, where Dr. Bimbi-Cole, the attending physician, placed two stitches on the cut, and assured my father that the artery had not been severed. I bear the mark of the stitches and cut to this day. Much later in life when girl friends would see the scar and would ask what happened I would reply that I tried to commit suicide and they would start probing what had gone wrong and why I wanted to do that. I would go along with their questions by inventing stories. Only when we had exhausted the exchange would I tell them the truth.

On another occasion, I was playing with a couple of friends on the front steps leading to the second-floor veranda. We had the habit of jumping from the steps to catch the topside of the veranda floor, and we would swing our body and then drop down. I had successfully completed this action for the first three steps. When I got to the fourth, I noticed the angle was sharp, but my friends had jumped from that step and had caught the top of the veranda. So, I decided to jump. My fingers could not hold on, and I lost my grip, causing me to fall and hit the back of my head on one of the steps. I suffered a concussion and lost consciousness immediately. When I regained it, some 20 minutes or so later, I was told, I found myself lying on my back on the ground, surrounded by my friends and Mrs. Nelson. It was raining lightly. They had laid me down in the rain to help me regain consciousness. I also discovered that I had hurt my wrist. Furthermore, the accident caused me to throw up the food that I had eaten that afternoon, a stew that I had enjoyed. But each time it was prepared after that incident, I became nauseated by the smell and would not eat it. My mother was away from the country with my sister, and my father was at work. When he came home, he was told what had happened. I was taken to the hospital the next day for observation, and my wrist was x-rayed. Papa and I were informed that I had cracked the bone, but it was not severe; and so, I did not wear a plaster cast, but I had to carry my right arm in a sling for about a month. If I did not wear the sling, my wrist would hurt in the vertical position. Another health issue pertained to my parents' predilection for Victorian health care treatments. I was given castor oil as a periodic bowel cleanser. But this time it made me sick, and so my parents stopped giving me castor oil. They replaced it with "glauber" salts, which also made me sick. Finally, they stopped the treatment entirely. Marmite paste, liver, and cod liver oil were other food or medicinal items that I detested. I could not stand the taste. It had been recommended by a health practitioner that I consume marmite for its vitamins either as a spread on a slice of bread or in liquid form. My mother would take a tablespoonful of marmite and pour hot water into a cup and mix the marmite and give it to me. When she was not looking, I would give it to Mrs. Nelson who would drink it. Eventually I stopped eating marmite and liver. I also experienced several bouts of malaria causing me to be absent for long periods during my first year at the Prince of Wales school.

On other occasions, the boys of Rasmusson Street would go fishing or swimming in the Congo River or stream to us, which was less than a mile from our house. We would say in Krio, (wi de go plohnj—we are going for a plunge.) One had to go down a hill path to get to the stream. Sometimes we crossed the stream and went up the other side of the valley as a shortcut to the Congo Cross main road. This was done usually in the dry season when the stream current was weak. However, during the rains, it became very risky to swim, and we never attempted to cross or enter certain sections of the stream where the current or flow was excessively strong. There were boys of the area who would follow the stream all the way to Congo Town where it entered the sea, but we never did that. It was reported that an alligator had been killed in that area, but the alligator was never displayed. We surmised that it was a ruse to prevent us from going to the stream.

By the time I was nine, I had started doing household chores. This included cleaning the bathroom and furniture of the house, making my bed and tidying up my room, sweeping and shining the floor, doing the laundry, and cooking, sewing, and painting, all under the supervision of my mother who also taught me how to bake. Each morning, we got up at 5:00am and we would complete house-cleaning chores before going to school. This included dusting the furniture in the living room area, cleaning the floor of the living room area, hallway, and dining room. I would then prepare tea for breakfast, take my bath, eat breakfast, and dash off to school around 7:00am. The school gate closed at 8:15am to be followed by roll call and assembly at 8:30am.

On Saturdays, Papa and I would do our weekend shopping. I was responsible for developing the shopping list with input from my mother. We would go first to Cold Storage, where he would get a set of provisions. Then he would continue to PZ (Paterson Zochonis) where he would get additional provisions. I used to cherish the cabin biscuits that he got from PZ, which were not always in regular supply. On those occasions when they were available, I would plead with him to get a lot. Following PZ, he would drive to Garrison Street market where he would get meat from his favourite butcher. He would then send me to the market women to get foo foo and other grocery items. I had my favourite vendors that I patronised. Nevertheless, others would try to woo my attention to buy their wares. We would conclude our shopping by stopping at Kingsway to get some ice cream and then drive home to 17 Rasmusson Street where my sister would be eagerly waiting for the ice cream.

At the Prince of Wales School, I was able to display my baking skills when I was charged with the responsibility of making the buns for a schoolhouse event. I was also good with my hands and could do mechanical repairs. Once Papa had to come and get me from school to fix his car when it broke down on Wilkinson Road, near Lumley. For pocket money from my mother, I would break laterite stones at the going rate of sixpence a bushel, granite stones went at nine pence a bushel. These survival skills became very useful to me when I was a student in the United States and Canada and as a young bachelor lecturer in Nigeria.

As I mentioned in a chapter above, my interest in cars had started with the incident of pouring water into the gasoline tank of my father's car at age four or five. As I grew older into my preteens, I became interested in driving his car. As fate would have it, he left for the United States and my mother depended on me to monitor the drivers whom she hired during my father's absence. I became very good friends with them. It was during this period that I learned how to drive a car. I was eleven going twelve. After a few attempts during which the car stalled when I released the clutch, I soon mastered the knack of slowly releasing the clutch and slowly increasing the pressure on the accelerator to move the car once it was in gear. I also mastered the knack of changing gears when the car was in motion. When my father returned from the United States, he found me driving his car. In the evenings, he would ask me to park his car in the garage. Of course, I took great pleasure in doing this. Word soon spread in the neighbourhood that I could drive my father's car, and I would take my friends in the neighbourhood on spins to the Recreation Grounds.

Due to my father being a United States trained graduate, we had the opportunity of hosting Americans who were visiting Sierra Leone. Dr. Lorenzo Turner, the famed Afro-American Linguist/Anthropologist was one such guest who came to Sierra Leone in October of 1951. Dr. Turner had been the first scholar to postulate a linguistic connection with Africa in the speech of the sea islanders, (Gullah/Geechee) living off the coast of South Carolina and Georgia. Further research had narrowed the link to West Africa, particularly the grain coast of Sierra Leone and Liberia. To confirm his hypothesis, Dr. Turner undertook field research that took him to Nigeria, Benin, Togo, Ghana, and Sierra Leone in the early fifties. While in Freetown, he recorded several artists/performers who told Krio stories, performed Krio songs, and conducted discussions on other aspects of Krio folklore. One resource person was Mr. Thomas Decker who, in the 1930's, had led the defence of Krio as a legitimate language, and had translated Shakespeare "As you Like It" and Julius Caesar" into Krio to demonstrate that the Krio language was capable of handling serious English Literature. I vividly recall artists coming to our residence at 3 Main Motor Road to perform. Dr. Turner had an old military type recorder that used wires for recording. Through him my parents and friends made a trip to Bunce Island to see the former slave castle. This was done under the direction of Dr M C F Easmon, curator of the Sierra Leone Museum. Dr Turner's research findings can now be accessed at the Smithsonian Institute in Washington DC. Little did I realise that I would undertake a similar research some twenty years later.

Another visitor of a longer duration was Miss Geneva Holmes, an Afro-American lady who came as a Fulbright Scholar in 1956 and lived with us for a year. Miss Holmes, through my father's connection, came as a visiting teacher at the Freetown Secondary School for Girls. As she lived with us, I had the opportunity to have several discussions with her about Higher Education in America and the idea of pursuing my university education in the United States started to take hold. She had taken a leave of absence from Fayetteville Teachers College in Fayetteville, North Carolina where she taught Social Studies. Later, she transferred to North Carolina Agricultural and Technical (A&T) State University in Greensboro where my father had been a professor in the 1920s following the completion of his master's degree at Columbia University in 1926. Miss Holmes was sociable, pleasant and gave a lot of her time to students who sought information on furthering their education in the United States. My cousin Violet Ebun Lewis (later Mrs. Porter) was one of the Sierra Leoneans who benefitted from her counsel. She was offered a scholarship to start a BA at North Carolina Agricultural and Technical College. Other beneficiaries were Teddy Jones and his cousin Rogers Jones who went to Tuskegee Institute in Alabama and later transferred to McGill and Ottawa Universities in Canada respectively.

As the fifties progressed, more houses were built on Rasmusson Street and Lower King Harman Road. This took place between 1954 and 1959. The Faulkners, the Bankole Jones, the Lukes, and the Cokers had moved to their homes on Lower King Harman Road by the end of 1955. Mr. and Mrs. Brimsley Johnson, Mrs. Macaulay and her daughters, Gladys and Dunstanette, had moved to their respective homes on Rasmusson Street by the end of 1956. Thus, there were more young people in the area. Among the newly arrived and living with the Faulkners was an attractive looking teenager by the name of Daphne Cline-Thomas, the younger sister of Mrs. Christine Faulkner and Teddy Cline-Thomas, a school mate at the Prince of Wales. She caught my fancy. In those days the way teenagers made friends with members of the opposite sex was to write letters. So, I wrote her a nice letter asking her to become my friend. She graciously accepted and I was very happy. Unfortunately, our growing friendship was interrupted when I departed for the United States of America to further my studies. Although we corresponded, a long-distance relationship was not practical for staying engaged. Fifty-two years later, I would meet her and her husband, Aneurin Solomon in London at a dinner in the home of John and Vanji Bankole-Jones. Age had taken its toll on us, but we both recognized each other.

The older boys were Alfred Bockry, Alfred Cole and me, and the younger boys comprised Teddy Stanley, Clifford Jones and his younger brother Louis Jones. Senior to the older boys were John Edward Bankole Jones and Joseph Stanley. Freddy Stanley had already left for his military studies at Sandhurst Military Academy in the United Kingdom. John and Joseph did not do much with us as they had other big boys' interests. There was also Tunji Luke, his sisters Bernadette and Isabella and younger brother, Michael. The boys had created the Brookfields Boys Club of which I was president (the girls had their own group). The club comprised mainly boys from the Brookfields area, Syke Street and Saint John. Those from Syke street included boys from the Columbus Thompson household (Charles Davis, Flavius Thompson, and others.) and my cousin Nathaniel (Ade) Broderick. We would hold our meetings at the St Edwards School on Sundays and Pa Feyi Cole was our mentor. Cricket and tennis became our favourite sports. We held our cricket practice at Saint Edwards School under the patronage of Reverend Father O'Sullivan, Principal of the School. I was a fast bowler together with Alfred Bockry and Bankole Saunders. Alfred Cole, was the wicket keeper, and we affectionately called him Godfrey Evans, after England's famous wicket keeper of the fifties and sixties. He was also nicknamed Ben Sisuh, after the famous Ghanaian national team football player of the fifties, whose hair style he imitated. On one occasion we played against the boys from Syke Street at the Recreation Grounds where we were all dressed in white, giving the appearance to spectators that this was serious cricket. To face the challenge presented by the Brookfields team, Syke Street incorporated players such as Stanley Frazer, a resident of Saint John, who became a renowned fast bowler as well as captain of the national cricket team of Sierra Leone. On balance, we had the better team, but we lost the game. As for tennis we played at the Brookfields City Council courts behind my house and at Dworzak courts on the Congo Cross Main Motor Road. Dr. Victor King, a renowned education officer, coached us. Other players who joined our group were Jestina Ashwood (later Mrs. Teddy Jones) and Veronica Shackleford (later Mrs. Gittens-Strong). In both tennis and cricket Louis Bankole Jones demonstrated that he was a rising star, and later played for Sierra Leone. However, the best among us was Alfred Bockry. He was so talented that he was selected in 1958 to play on the Sierra Leone Cricket team that toured the Gambia. He was the youngest member of the team at the age of sixteen.

Chapter: 8

The Struggle for Independence - An Overview

In 1884, European leaders met in Berlin, Germany, to carve up the African continent to suit their imperial interests. The major players were Great Britain, France, Portugal, Spain, Germany, and Belgium. In terms of landmass, Britain and France acquired the largest portions. The French dominated West Africa and Britain and Germany dominated East and Southern Africa. The Hut Tax War in 1898 kick-started African resistance to British colonialism in Sierra Leone. The colonial government had imposed a hut tax to raise revenue to administer the colony. The levying of taxes was met with opposition under the dynamic leadership of Bai Bureh, a famous Temne Chief. The war resulted in the deaths of British civilians and white American missionaries as well as Krios who were civilian employees recruited to serve British imperial interests. Although the British captured Bai Bureh and eventually quelled the revolt, the seeds of opposition had, nevertheless, been sown. Bai Bureh's leadership would serve as an example for launching opposition to British rule in Sierra Leone and European imperialism in general in Africa. Activities of this nature gave birth to the twentieth century independence movements that crystallised in the forties, fifties, and sixties. In Sierra Leone, ITA Wallace Johnson, a trade union activist and politician, had become a thorn in the side of the British in the late 1930's. He was a gifted speaker who drew large crowds to his public lectures where he denounced the injustices of the colonial government in their treatment of Africans.

The return of African soldiers who had fought for the British during the Second World War to their homelands contributed immensely to the creation of a national awareness in the struggle for independence. In the Gold Coast, for example, which later became Ghana, these soldiers had sparked off riots in Accra in 1947 during which they protested bitterly against economic and political conditions and the way Ghanaians civil servants were being treated by their British administrators. They complained about the contradiction in fighting to save the British Empire while their people were not free in their own country. In colonial Africa, for example, highly trained African civil servants were discriminated against in terms of salary and appointments by their colonial counterparts even though the latter were less qualified in terms of training and experience. Kwame Nkrumah, who would later lead the Gold Coast to Independence in 1957 capitalised on the national consciousness generated by the soldiers. He had received his education from the United States of America where he had identified himself with the struggle of blacks against segregation. He was influenced by the teachings of the famous African American educationist cum politician, philosopher, and diplomat, Edward Wilmot Blyden, and by the Jamaican Nationalist, Marcus Garvey, who advocated the return of African Americans to Africa. Kwame Nkrumah, a pan Africanist, and believer of Blyden's doctrine of "African Personality", would promote these policies by making Ghana a haven for African Americans when he became Prime Minister of Ghana. One of the notable Black Americans who immigrated to Ghana was William Edward Burghardt Dubois, a formidable academic, prolific writer, historian and political activist, who died in 1963 and was buried in Ghana.

In Sierra Leone, Trade Unionists protests took place in 1955 when Freetown was gripped with riots triggered by the high cost of living and low wages paid to workers by the colonial Government. The demonstrations, which resulted in the looting of merchant stores owned by Lebanese traders and the killing of rioters, could not be controlled by the police and the military had to be mobilised to restore order.

One of the victims killed had been a British military officer, whose death must have incurred the wrath of the British colonial authorities. Politically, the quest for self-rule started in 1951 with the formation of the Legislative Council where Sierra Leoneans became participants. The national movement towards independence gained momentum in 1957 with the formation of political parties. The Sierra Leone Peoples party, under the leadership of Dr. Milton Margai, a British trained Medical Officer, won the first national elections in 1957; and Dr. Margai, as Chief Minister, led Sierra Leone to independence talks with the British Government in the late 1950s. Ghana's independence in 1957 reinforced the anti-colonial struggle in Sierra Leone as well as in West Africa. When Ghana achieved her independence on March 6, 1957, it was a joyous day in Sierra Leone. At the Prince of Wales School, the Principal dismissed students at midday to honour Ghana's achievement. In 1960, Nigeria with the largest population in Black Africa became independent from Great Britain and Sierra Leone followed suit in 1961, becoming the 100th member of the United Nations. The Gambia would become independent in 1965. French colonies had become independent in 1960; and between 1960 and 1965, most African nations had become independent from their European colonial masters.

PART TWO: NORTH AMERICA

Chapter: 9

Sailing the Atlantic, North America Bound

On August 1, 1959, I sailed on the Motor Vessel (MV) Aureol, together with my father, for the United States of America via the United Kingdom. This ship, the flagship of Elder Dempster lines, had been introduced in 1951 to augment the number of passenger vessels provided by Elder Dempster lines for transporting passengers to and from West Africa to the United Kingdom. It was more modern than her sister ships, the MV Accra and MV Apapa. I was pleased that we were travelling on the Aureol and not her older sister ships. I was on my way to start my university education at Otterbein University in Westerville, Ohio, and Papa was on his way to take up a Fulbright Professorship at North Carolina Agricultural and Technical (A&T) State University in Greensboro, North Carolina. Tears came to my eyes as the vessel pulled away from the dock. Indeed, it was a very sad day for me as we bade farewell to my mother and sister as well as to other relatives and family friends who had come to see Papa and me off. Not knowing when I would see them again added to my sadness. An hour later we had sailed past the Cape Lighthouse, a famous landmark in Sierra Leone, exited the estuary of the Sierra Leone River and on our way to join the Atlantic Ocean. In Sierra Leone folklore, "to Cross the Cape" was a way of saying that one had physically left the shores of Sierra Leone by sea on a mission abroad. It was a popular saying amongst the youth. The vibrations of the ship caused me to start feeling seasick, and I was surprised that I would feel that way so soon after we had departed Freetown. I thought if I were going to become sea-sick, it would happen on the high seas, maybe when we got to the Bay of Biscay whose dreaded storms I had heard about. On board the boat was a young Sierra Leonean student by the name of Mavis

Peacock who was travelling to the United Kingdom to further her education. There was also a Mr. Tunde Coker who was going to study Art in Italy and another Sierra Leonean lady by the name of Harris who was pursuing higher studies in the United Kingdom. We all became friends, as we ate and socialised together. There were also other African passengers from Ghana and Nigeria whom we befriended. Accordingly, our sad departure subsequently turned into pleasant social gatherings. Our only Port of Call before we reached Liverpool was Las Palmas in the Canary Islands, off the coast of Northwest Africa. What a relief to see land again after being at sea for five days! I remember going out on deck early that morning and seeing a massive piece of land rising in the horizon. I quickly returned to my cabin and beckoned Mr. Coker, and we both returned to the deck to behold the sight. Later we went sightseeing on the island. It was a good feeling to set foot on *terra firma*. We hired a taxi, and the driver took us sightseeing around the island. One site was a cathedral where the taxi driver claimed Christopher Columbus had worshipped during one of his trips to the Americas. I bought a Parker fountain pen of which I was proud, as it was a status symbol in Sierra Leone among schoolboys, only to discover when I got to the United States, much to my disappointment, that it was a fake copy. The remainder of the trip was uneventful including the much-dreaded crossing of the Bay of Biscay. On the tenth day of leaving Sierra Leone, we arrived at Liverpool where we disembarked, having passed the night in thick fog. I saw faces that I recognized in the crowd of Sierra Leoneans that had come to greet arriving family members and friends as well as to receive letters and food items. After completing formalities, we boarded the train for Euston Station in London. Four hours later we were in London, where again I recognized faces of Sierra Leoneans who had come to welcome family members and or friends. I bade farewell to my Sierra Leonean passenger friends, and we promised to stay in touch. Papa and I spent two weeks in London where he had work to complete before arriving in the United States of America. He had a suit made for me as an advance gift for my birthday on September 15. The suit lasted four years by which time I had outgrown it. While in London, I hooked up with two old school mates, Philip Gage and Nicholas Palmer, whose friendship dated from our days at the Government Model and the Prince of Wales Schools. Philip had departed Sierra Leone in 1957 to further his education in the United Kingdom and Nick had left in 1958 to do likewise. It was a joyous reunion. Papa invited them to lunch at a nice restaurant. As we dined, they asked me a lot of questions about life in Freetown and news about other classmates and girlfriends. Following lunch, they took me sightseeing, Buckingham Palace, Houses of Parliament, etc. As we walked, we passed a store where Frankie Avalon's song, "Venus," was being played. When I heard the song, I started to sing along; and suddenly Nick said to me, "You mean this song is already in Freetown!" I was surprised by the question. I responded "yes, for about a year", and quickly reminded him that, in case he had forgotten, there was a BBC Radio Service in Freetown that played current hits before he left, and that it was still functioning after his departure, and that it was still functioning after my departure." We all laughed. That evening we said farewell to one another as Papa and I were leaving for the United States in a few days, and we would not have the opportunity to see them again. We promised to stay in touch. Papa also introduced me to family friends: Aunty Beatrice Renner and her daughter Miss Phyllis and to an English couple, Mr. and Mrs. Singleton of Kent. I also met their younger son, Christopher, with whom I had a pen pal relationship. Papa had met the Singletons as students at Cambridge University in the nineteen thirties. We sailed on the RMS, Parthia, from Liverpool for New York City on August 29, arriving on the evening of September 5. The third day at sea, we experienced very harsh weather, which caused the ship to roll. That morning I felt sick, nauseated, unstable, and drained, and did not make it to breakfast. Lunchtime, I summoned courage and made it to the dining room only to find it practically empty. The waiter told me that there had been no one for breakfast. After that experience the rest of the sailing was fine.

It was a spectacular sight to behold the skyline of New York City all beautifully lit as we pulled into the harbour on the evening of September 5th. For about a day and a half until our arrival, we could see dolphins following the ship. We were told by one of the ship officials that sighting dolphins meant we were getting closer to land. During our crossing of the Atlantic, I made friends with some of the passengers who took an interest in me, thus giving me the opportunity to question them about college life and living in the United States in general. They were for the most part young Americans who had spent the summer in Europe and were returning home. They were energetic and full of life. There had also been parties on the ship which brought passengers together and where I learned popular American songs such as: "Oh When the Saints Go Marching In," "Ain't she Sweet!" and "Tea for Two." Although we arrived at dusk, one could sense that passengers wanted off the ship that same evening, even though the ship authorities gave us the option of staying the night and departing the next day. I'm not sure whether anyone took up the offer. Following the completion of formalities, Papa and I got a taxi to take us to the International House at Riverside Drive where he had made reservations. This building, I later learned from him, had been established by John D. Rockefeller, the philanthropist, to promote better relationships between Americans and foreign students, and that he, my father, had stayed there when he was a student at Columbia University in the mid nineteen twenties. After we checked in, we decided to go out to eat as we were hungry and all food service at the International House had ended by the time we arrived. We ended up in a small restaurant where he ordered baked chicken, mashed potatoes, and gravy with vegetables, and I ordered hamburgers and French fries to be followed by dessert - my first introduction to American fast food. As we walked back to the International House around midnight, I noticed that there were young children still playing in the streets - an unlikely event in Freetown. I wondered why their parents would allow for such a thing to take place!

Papa had first arrived in New York City in August of 1920 to commence his studies at Otterbein College (now Otterbein University) in Westerville, Ohio. He had entered New York through Ellis Island, the principal gateway for immigrants to the United States at that time. In the 1930s, the United States Immigration Service stopped using Ellis Island as the entry point for immigrants and thus my arrival was not at Ellis Island. Nevertheless, I recently discovered records of Papa's arrival on Ellis Island. He had sailed from Freetown on July 13 on an Elder Dempster cargo ship, New Brunswick, which docked at Ellis Island on August 2 from where he proceeded to Westerville, Ohio.[18]

While in New York City Papa took me sightseeing. We visited President Ulysses Grant's tomb and Columbia University, his alma mater, which were close by, Riverside Drive Church where we worshipped, Saint John the Divine Cathedral, the United Nations, the Empire State Building, and Sarah Lawrence College where he attended a Fulbright meeting. International news had to do with Chairman Nikita Khrushchev of the Soviet Union who had also arrived in the US to give a speech at the United Nations. He caused much commotion when he took off his shoes and hit the table to underscore a point. Several occurrences caught my eye during our stay in New York City, for example, huge trucks with brushes sweeping the streets, people having their shoes shined in public places, the noisy subway trains and people

---

[18]. "Ellis Island-Free Port of New York Passenger Records Search," accessed March 7, 2013, http://www.ellisisland.org/search/viewTextManifest,asp?MID=1 5554...

rushing and bumping into one another as if they were chickens running around with their heads cut off. I was also keen on popular music and two songs that caught my ear were Bobby Darin's *"Mack the Knife"*, which was high on the music chart and whose lyrics I later discovered had been taken from Bertolt Brecht's "*Threepenny Opera*." The other was the Everly Brothers *"Til I Kissed You"*. Bobby Darin was new to me, but the Everly Brothers I knew from Sierra Leone, where they had a strong following amongst the youth with such hits *as "Bye Love, "Wake up Little Susie, "Dream" and "Devoted to You."* A family friend from Sierra Leone who called upon us, was Joy Smythe-Macaulay (now Mrs. Samake). It was splendid to see her, and she gave me tips as to what to expect when I started my college life. She had arrived in the US some two years earlier to pursue her university education at Bryn Mawr University.

On September 13, I boarded a Greyhound Bus and travelled overnight to the capital city of Ohio, Columbus, en route to Otterbein University, located in Westerville, Ohio, twelve miles separating the two municipalities. An official from the University, I think his name was Tom Lehman, picked me up at the Greyhound Station who drove me to my dormitory where I met my roommate, John Moorhead, an American student from Saint Thomas, in the US Virgin Islands. John had written to me while I was in Freetown to introduce himself as the University had informed him that I was going to be his roommate. He informed me that he had lived in Liberia for two years where his father, a Medical Doctor, worked with the United States Government Point Four Programme, the precursor to the United States Agency for International Development, and while there he had met Dr. John Karefa-Smart, a Sierra Leonean doctor who worked for the World Health Organisation and a graduate of Otterbein University. John and his family had left Liberia for Teheran, Iran, in 1957, where his father had been assigned. It was through this Liberia connection with Dr. Karefa-Smart that his family had been told of Otterbein

University. I wrote back to John thanking him for his letter and informing him that I knew Dr. John Karefa–Smart, and that I looked forward to meeting him in Westerville.

Chapter: 10

"In a Quiet Peaceful Village"

My knowledge of Otterbein University and the "village" of Westerville had started with my father. He had told my sister and me about his stay in America. For example, before going to America, we both knew the Otterbein Love Song, which starts with the line "In a Quiet Peaceful Village" and the names of some of its historical personalities; some of whom were still alive when I arrived in September of 1959. The University prides itself as being one of the first institutions of higher education in Ohio that admitted African American and women students. In the intervening years between my father's graduation in 1924 and 1960, other Sierra Leoneans had graduated from Otterbein. These included Ross Lohr (1927), Richard Kelfa-Caulker (1935), John Karefa-Smart (1940) who gave the Commencement Address in June 1961, John Akar (1951), Max Bailor (1953), Ademu-John (1956), Victor Sumner (1959), Amelia Georginia Caulker (1959), and Lloyd Bailor (1960). All these Sierra Leoneans had returned home to work for the Government of Sierra Leone in various capacities and made significant contributions. The only exceptions were Ross Lohr and Ademu John. Ross Lohr remained in the United States where he became a Professor of Education at Hampton Institute in Virginia and Ademu John worked in Dayton, Ohio. Imodale Kelfa-Caulker (now Mrs. Caulker-Burnett and daughter of Mr. and Mrs. Richard Kelfa-Caulker) and I were the two Sierra Leoneans that entered the university in 1959. Raymond Bailor followed in 1960 and Miatta Koroma, Maude Fraser and Frederick Noah arrived in the autumn of 1961. Frederick, whom I had known in Freetown, roomed with me during his freshman year.

The integration of public schools, housing and other

public facilities together with the exercise of the franchise by African Americans constituted the focus of the Civil Rights Struggle in the fifties and sixties in the United States. President Truman had set the stage in the late forties by integrating the United States armed forces and this example would carry over into the fifties through the Supreme Court's decision in 1954 that overturned the "separate but equal doctrine" in the case: "Brown versus the Board of Education of Topeka, Kansas." This landmark decision, which came into effect after sixty years, reversed the court's verdict of 1896 that had upheld the doctrine in the case, "Plessy versus Ferguson." The fragile civil rights truce was jolted in 1955 with the brutal murder by whites of a young black youth, Emmitt Till, aged 14, in Mississippi. It was alleged that the youth, a native of Chicago who was visiting relatives in Mississippi, had whistled at a white woman, and was gruesomely beaten to death by incensed whites for his "transgression." Rosa Parks, a black woman, would refuse to give up her seat to a white man when asked to do so by the white driver of the bus in which she was riding. In 1957, President Dwight Eisenhower federalized Arkansas national guards and ordered them to escort nine black students to integrate a High School in Little Rock, Arkansas, where they had been refused admission. In 1960, John Fitzgerald Kennedy (JFK) was elected President of the United States, and he would give moral leadership to the civil rights movement by giving national television broadcasts condemning segregation such as his speech on June 11, 1963, in which he discussed how segregation affects education, public safety and international relations. JFK used his brother Robert Kennedy, who was the Attorney General, to integrate the University of Alabama and Georgia using federal troops. That same evening (June 11, 1963), Medgar Evers, a civil rights activist in Mississippi would be gunned down by white supremacists. President Kennedy would make his mark on the African continent by supporting the struggle for independence - a major policy-break with the European colonial powers that were also allies of the United States. For example, his backing of African independence had started when he was still a Senator by supporting Ahmed Sekou Toure's break with France in 1958 to establish the Republic of Guinea. Furthermore, to attract African students to the United States, he arranged for scholarships to be offered to them to pursue their studies. This support for African independence and the provision of scholarships to Africans to pursue their higher education made him America's most admired President in Africa at the time. His biggest legacy to Africa was the creation of the Peace Corps, which gave young American students the opportunity to offer their skills to Africans and other citizens of the developing world. This approach was a direct way of promoting America to the third world at the grass root level. For example, Peace Corps volunteers would be assigned to remote areas in Third World countries where they interacted with town's people and villagers. To enhance their interactions, they also learned to speak local languages and eat local foods. The promotion of America in Africa produced two important results: First, through the exchange, more African students started to come to the United States for their higher education—thereby slowly breaking the colonial grip that European nations, (mainly the United Kingdom, France, and Portugal) had on Africa. Second, the Peace Corps provided benefits to the American people by developing a cadre of young energetic Americans, knowledgeable about Africa and the third world, who were recruited into the State Department and the United States Agency for International Development.

The freedom rides movement to integrate lunch counters would start in Greensboro, North Carolina led by students from North Carolina Agricultural and Technical State University. In August 1963, Dr. Martin Luther King would lead the March on Washington, where he delivered his famous speech "I have a Dream." A month later four black girls died from the bombing of the 16th Street Baptist Church in Birmingham, Alabama by white supremacists of the Ku Klux Klan; and the civil rights activist and Black Muslim Leader, Malcolm X, was preaching to black audiences to take up arms to defend themselves against physical attacks by white supremacists. President Kennedy would be assassinated in November of 1963 in Dallas Texas, an incident that stunned the moral fibre of the nation. He would be replaced by Vice President Johnson who upheld the struggle for civil rights by taking the lead in getting the Civil Rights Act of 1964 and the Civil Rights Voting Act of 1965 passed by Congress. The Reverend Martin Luther King would lead additional marches in Birmingham and Selma, Alabama advocating for more civil rights for blacks. My future father-in-law, Dr. William Henry Fitzjohn, Charge d'Affaires of the Embassy of Sierra Leone and a graduate of Lincoln and Columbia Universities, was refused service at a Howard Johnson restaurant on Route 40 in Hyattsville, Maryland, because of his race. This caused a diplomatic incident for which President Kennedy invited him to the White House to offer an apology on behalf of the United States Government and people. Meanwhile, on the continent of Africa, African States were becoming independent from their European colonial masters; and this change would serve as fuel to energise the civil rights movement in the United States. In October 1962, a third world war almost broke out between the United States and the Soviet Union over the Cuban Missile Crisis. Skilful diplomacy by the Kennedy administration resolved the conflict. The struggle for civil rights by African Americans and the fight to stop the spread of communism were the topics that dominated the racial and political landscape in the United States when I arrived in Westerville, a peaceful small mid-western town in central Ohio.

I embarked on my freshman studies which comprised mainly fulfilling required core courses in the areas of the Humanities, Social Sciences and Pure Sciences, Languages and Physical Education. Each student was assigned a faculty advisor with whom he/she would discuss his/her workload and academic goals. Because of my interest in the Sciences at the Prince of Wales School in Sierra Leone, I thought I would like to major in the Pure Sciences with a pre-med emphasis, but later, I discovered that my true passion was in the Humanities and Social Sciences. At the start of my second year, I switched emphasis to the Humanities, Social Sciences, and Languages, concentrating on courses in English Literature, American History, European History, American Diplomatic History, International Relations, American Government and four years of French Language and Literature. My aim was to enter the diplomatic service of the Sierra Government, following the path of Victor Sumner, an Otterbein graduate from Sierra Leone. On completing Otterbein, Victor had gone to L'Universite Laval, in Quebec City, Canada to pursue a master's degree in French, and would later join the Sierra Leone Government's Diplomatic Service as a civil servant in the Ministry of Foreign Affairs.

One academic exercise to which I had to adjust was the frequency of tests. Students were always studying for tests in addition to mid-term tests and finals at the end of a semester. It was a way of continually staying mentally fit for undertaking an intellectual exercise at any time. The frequency was unlike the European system where tests were mainly at the end of the term. Furthermore, I also had to adjust to the system of objective testing (i.e., answering to true or false questions) which was new to me. I was accustomed to writing essays to questions. I soon realised that the objective tests focused more on demonstrating one's knowledge of factual matters and not necessarily on how well one can write. This type of testing also made it easy for the tests to be graded. Another new discovery was the term or research paper, an exercise I had not been exposed to in my secondary school education. However, I discovered that it was a useful application as it encouraged the sharpening of one's reading, analytical and organisational skills; and that the more one did it, the better one became. Since Otterbein was a small institution with less than 1,200 students, there were lots of opportunities to meet with one's professors for assistance and some professors' mentored students by holding informal discussions in their homes. Academic assistance was also provided by upper class men (third year and fourth year students - juniors and seniors) through studying sessions at fraternities or sororities. Two extra mural areas of interest that I brought with me from Sierra Leone were my love for singing and playing sports. I joined the men's glee club my freshman year and was a member all through my four years. I enjoyed the tours that we took in the spring, which gave me the opportunity to visit other cities and towns in and out of Ohio. One year we travelled as far west as Saint Louis, Missouri, and another year we visited the New England States of New Hampshire, Massachusetts, Vermont, and Connecticut. We sang in churches and community centres, including the rotunda of the capitol building in Scranton, Pennsylvania, where Governor Scranton received us. Dr. Shackson, the Music Director, avoided tours in the South because of the racial situation and undertook tours in the Northeast and Midwest. Nevertheless, an ugly incident took place in southwestern, Ohio, where John Moorhead and I were refused service at a restaurant. In general, I noticed that black students were better received by white Americans when the latter found out that they were Africans or foreigners and not black Americans. Athletic wise, I was too small to play American football, and soccer, which I played well, was not yet a collegiate men's sport. I contented myself with tennis, which I enjoyed, and played on the fraternity team and later Otterbein's varsity team. My father had been an avid athlete at Otterbein and had set his mark in track for which he received a gold watch. I was trying to emulate him.

Social life at Otterbein was built around fraternities and sororities and the bid for pledges started early in one's freshman year. By the time Christmas vacation arrived, we, members of the freshman class, were already members of different fraternities or sororities. The bond that we had established with our freshman classmates in the dormitories was now broken. The Greeks, as the fraternities/sororities were known, organised social events as hayrides, dances, pledge parties, and major college events such as Homecoming, etc. My freshman Year I was elected to be the Jump Week King, a memorable event that I will treasure. (This is an occasion when female students invite male students out for a social function such as a dance. I was one of five candidates, representing my fraternity "Phi Kappa Phi-- Country Club" who competed for the position of Jump Week King, having been elected by female students.) In my junior year, I served as a dormitory counsellor.

As foreign students from Africa we were objects of curiousity. Some of our American classmates were from towns where there were hardly any blacks or had never met a black person, let alone an African. The fact that we could speak and write the Queen's English was an enigma to them. Some of them found it hard to reconcile us against the sensational contrived images that they had been accustomed to seeing in movies such as Tarzan and Jane, where "African natives" rarely featured or were portrayed running around uttering funny sounds and being sparsely clothed. In these movies white characters interacted with one another but not with Africans, although the setting was supposed to be in Africa. On the other side of the coin, the effect of this portrayal was not different from the way Africans believed that the United States was full of cowboys and Indians and gangsters robbing banks, as this is what was depicted in the films that they saw of the United States in Africa. If a difference could be identified, it stemmed from Africans seeing films of America made by Americans, while Americans saw films of Africa made by Americans. Africans were not the producers of "African films". They were not telling their stories. Indeed, no story was being told by them. They were rather passive consumers, while Americans were both active producers and consumers. Furthermore, Africa's image of being wild and uncivilised was reinforced in the lyrics of the Kingston Trio's song, "They are rioting in Africa," which was popular in the music chart and sung to us by our American colleagues. I would rebut by substituting the lyrics of "God Bless America" with "God Bless Africa." But as the sixties progressed, rioting in the United States, triggered by the struggle for civil rights and protests the war in Vietnam, had become the order of the day. Now the situation had been turned upon its head. "They were rioting in America."

The African foreign students were often invited to give lectures at churches about "Africa" (Sierra Leone) and about the contributions made by the Evangelical United Brethren Church in Sierra Leone. I would begin my talk by making it clear to my audience that I was talking specifically about Sierra Leone and not about Africa in general. At summer camps the ignorance of Africa was even more profound. But this was to be expected, as the campers were mainly young students who had no knowledge of Africa other than the sensational stereotypic images seen in movies or on television. Displaying ignorance or contempt for Africa was not limited to whites.

African Americans were also guilty of this behaviour. I recall an incident at a black institution in Ohio, where we (Sierra Leoneans from Otterbein and Sierra Leoneans from this institution) were insulted by some African American students. We (Sierra Leoneans from Otterbein) had been invited to a social gathering to commemorate Sierra Leone's first Independence anniversary by our Sierra Leone colleagues of the university. As we walked through the campus to the venue for the event, donned in our African dress, we were told to take off our smelly pyjamas and gowns, and go back to Africa. Our Sierra Leonean colleagues reported the incident to the Dean of Students. The Dean apologised on behalf of the students, stating that they came from deprived backgrounds and did not know any better. We accepted her apology and the matter ended there. We were, nevertheless, stunned by the behaviour. African students attending colleges in other parts of the

United States were also victims of such behaviour from African American students. A Sierra Leonean student friend of mine told me of an incident in Washington DC where he and another Sierra Leonean student were chased by African American students who were shouting at them to, "go cut off that hair from your head." This was the age when to be "clean" African American males wore their hair very short with well shaven cheeks; and females had their hair "stretched" out with a hot comb. Ironically, that style would be frowned upon in the mid-to-late sixties with the advent of the Afro-bush hairstyle, (au naturel as it was called). The term "Negro" would be replaced by "Black," and the slogan "Black is beautiful" became the emblem of Black pride.

An intellectual challenge that remains to be addressed is to make Americans understand that, unlike Australia, which is a continent and a country, Africa is not a country but a continent, comprising over 50 independent countries with a variety of languages, cultures, and vegetation. Accordingly, what happens in country (X) does not necessarily happen in country (Y). In the immigration documents prepared for my father, the immigration officer on Ellis Island, in 1920, had written "Africa" for country and "Sierra Leone" for town/city.[19] Unfortunately, this "intellectual laziness or bias" has not changed as the American mass media continues to present Africa as a country fifty plus years after independence. Some Americans are stunned to learn that Egypt, Tunisia, Libya and the ancient Roman ruins in Morocco are in Africa. Furthermore, the contributions of

---

[19]

"Ellis Island-Free Port of New York Passenger Records Search," accessed March 7, 2013,
http://www.ellisisland.org/search/shipManifest,asp?MID=15554 6223608:

the Moors to European civilization, following eight hundred years of occupancy of the Iberian Peninsula, are hardly known. To counter this lack of specificity, African students must also take the responsibility to improve the intellectual knowledge of Americans on Africa by not falling into the trap of talking about Africa in vague or imprecise terms or as if it were a country. Rather, they should educate their American friends by being intellectually specific. Moreover, they should be ready to explain such conundrums as South Africa, Central African Republic; and Namibia which was once called Southwest Africa.

On the positive side, I soon discovered that there was dignity in manual labour, that having a degree or being lettered did not make Americans shy away from manual work, but rather they took great pride in dirtying their hands to undertake difficult physical jobs. Indeed, the greatness of America had come from its blue-collar class of workers, and that Americans dedicated a special day in the year "labour Day" in recognition of the monumental contributions of its labour work force. This was very much unlike the situation in Sierra Leone where a lettered man would frown on manual labour. Some of my American classmates did odd jobs in the town of Westerville, and during the summer, to augment their funds for tuition and other college expenses, did construction and road building jobs - a topic that my father had discussed with me, emphasising he had done manual jobs while a student at Otterbein. It was known as "working your way through school," as opposed to being on a scholarship or being supported by one's parents. For example, I recall a student friend who worked as a security warden on the campus. His work required doing rounds in the dead of night, rain, sleet, or snow, checking on buildings every two hours. I thought it was a hazardous job for a student. During the long summer vacation, I worked on the college's maintenance crew doing janitorial work, cleaning, and waxing floors, laying tiles, painting dormitories, or raking leaves. When the college was in session, I worked in the library, and as an assistant in the French language lab. At my Fraternity, I washed dishes, pots, and pans in exchange for my meals. It was not difficult for me to do these jobs as I had been accustomed to doing manual work, under the tutelage of my mother, while growing up in Sierra Leone.

A student by the name of Donald Marshal, whom I had met in my Botany class, befriended me. He invited me home for Thanksgiving and introduced me to his family and church friends. I soon realised that Thanksgiving was a big American celebration that was cherished as citizens gave special thanks to the Almighty for benefits and good health during the past year. While at the Marshalls, I experienced my first snow from which we built a snowman. Close family friends of the Marshalls were Clive and Kate Shaffer of Midvale, Ohio, who also took an interest in me. They invited me home for Christmas that year, my first in America. It was a memorable occasion as I helped the family members; Claudia, Marjorie, Hazel, and their Aunt Betty decorate the Christmas tree and partook in the singing of Christmas carols. I continued to visit with the Shaffer family and when my graduation occurred, they drove to Westerville to support me. My sister, Ore Emma Broderick, would continue the tradition that I had established with them when she attended Otterbein. Unfortunately, I lost touch with the Shaffers during the late sixties, but recently discovered with great sorrow from Donald Marshal that Clive and Kate Shaffer were killed in a head-on road accident some ten years ago. On a happier note, I have reconnected with their daughters, Claudia, Marjorie, and Hazel who are now grandparents.

On April 27, 1961, Sierra Leone became independent. Imodale Kelfa-Caulker, Raymond Bailor and I, the three Sierra Leoneans, travelled to Washington DC to take part in the independence celebrations, organised by the Sierra Leone Embassy. Mr. and Mrs. J. C. James, members of the "Friends of Sierra Leone Committee," hosted Raymond and me while Imodale stayed with Dr. and Mrs. William Fitzjohn, family friends of my parents. Dr. Fitzjohn, Charge d'Affaires at the Sierra Leone Embassy, accorded me the honour of hoisting the Sierra Leone flag at the ceremony. I also had the honour of meeting Assistant Secretary of State for African Affairs, G. Mennen-Williams, the first American to hold this newly created position in the Kennedy Administration, and other dignitaries from the Washington diplomatic scene as well as numerous Sierra Leonean students who lived in the Washington DC area or neighbouring States. At Otterbein, Imodale and I gave a copy of the newly composed Sierra Leone national anthem to Dr. Lee Shackson, Director of the Men and Women Glee Clubs. In a combined performance, both clubs lustily sang the song, as part of their Spring Concert programme, making the event a truly memorable experience. An American musical icon, the famous African American Spiritual Singer, Mariam Anderson, performed at Otterbein my senior year. Besides her tremendous voice, she had gained prominence in the late thirties when the daughters of the American Revolution annulled her performance in Constitutional Hall because of her race, prompting Mrs. Eleanor Roosevelt, wife of President Franklin D. Roosevelt, to resign her membership from the organisation. I had the good fortune to meet her at a reception following her performance.

In June of 1963, I graduated from Otterbein with a double major in History-Government as one major and French as the other. Other close friends who graduated included Imodale Kelfa-Caulker, John Moorhead and Jean Victor Poulard, a French student. Our Commencement Speaker was the Honourable Richard Kelfa-Caulker, Sierra Leone's Ambassador to the United States of America. My cousin, Violet Ebun Lewis who lived in Washington, DC also attended the ceremony. We, the minority and foreign students, celebrated the occasion at the home of Mr. and Mrs. (Howard and Helen) Ware, an African American couple, of Worthington, Ohio. It was an all-nighter. At the event I met an African American female student at the Ohio State University who would become a friend. She and other

African Americans had been invited to the party by our host and hostess as an opportunity for Africans to meet African Americans. At Otterbein, the availability of black female students was far and few between. But this does not mean that white girls were available to befriend, as interracial dating was tabooed. At the most, there were a dozen black students, (Africans and African Americans combined) the gender ratio was one to one and this comprised approximately six males and six females. Matching opposite partners was not necessarily easy, given personalities. I dated two black female students, an African American and later a Sierra Leonean.

A memorable social event was spent during Easter weekend of 1962 in Cleveland Ohio as the guests of Mary Hall, an African American student at Otterbein. Her family invited Imodale, Miatta, Freddy, John, and me (Raymond was unable to go) to Cleveland to meet relatives and friends. We had a super time touring the city and partying late into the evening. Members of our social group unanimously agreed that the event in Cleveland and the graduation party were our best social gatherings while we were students at Otterbein.

Academically, Otterbein proved to be an excellent experience. Given its small size, students were able to benefit from this attribute, as professors were friendly and accessible. Furthermore, the town was located twelve miles from the bustling city of Columbus and this distance was to our advantage. There was not much distraction and to go anywhere outside of Westerville, one needed a car or catch a bus which was infrequent. These limitations further strengthened the urge to study and to stay out of mischief, although my fraternity, Country Club, got into serious trouble for cutting down the goal post at Capital University, Otterbein's main rival, following an Otterbein football victory. Such occurrences, nevertheless, were far and few between. I recently visited the University for my 50th graduation anniversary, my fifth visit since graduation. I was truly impressed with the development that had taken place on the campus over the last 50 years. The campus had extended, a new library and science hall had been built together with new dormitories and a sports complex. Furthermore, a Mass Communication Programme had been established, a new Student Centre opened, and a first-class Equine Programme started. In addition, the staff has been improved with more PhDs., and the college is now a university (Otterbein University) that offers graduate programmes in several areas. The university is listed as one of the top small institutions of higher education in the Midwest of the United States.

Chapter: 11

"Quebec Oui, Ottawa Non" and "Vive le Quebec Libre."

The first utterance was by young French-Canadian demonstrators and the second by General Charles de Gaulle, the President of France. I had gone to Universite Laval, one of Canada's oldest universities to pursue a master's programme in French. The university was in Quebec City. I arrived at a time when there was much political turmoil in French Canada concerning the precarious relationship between the Province of Quebec and the Federal Government in Ottawa. The movement to separate the Province of Quebec from the rest of Canada was very much alive. It was characterized by young French Canadians of the Front de Liberation Quebecoise (FLQ) demonstrating and setting off bombs in postal boxes and at public monuments, mainly in the French-Canadian Cities of Montreal and Quebec. I had left the United States of America, rife with civil rights demonstrations, only to arrive in a country north of the border, in the Province of Quebec, plagued with demonstrations that sought to "redress" political and economic rights.

In 1964, Queen Elizabeth accompanied by her husband, His Royal Highness Prince Philip, visited Quebec City. The Queen, as Head of the British Commonwealth of Nations, was fulfilling her role as Queen of Canada as the Federal Government had invited her to Canada. The Queen's visit triggered violent demonstrations by university students in Quebec City, and Montreal, where they could be heard chanting, "Quebec Oui, Ottawa Non" and "God *Shave* the Queen." As the visit occurred on the heels of the Kennedy assassination in November of 1963, the Canadian Government took precautionary measures to prevent such an incident occurring in Canada. I was rooming in a house located on Rue St Louis, one of the popular streets in Old Quebec and where the Queen's motorcade was going to pass. Agents of the Canadian Mounted police occupied all the rooms, facing both sides of the street. Fortunately, my room did not face the street and I did not have to move. Nevertheless, I wanted to see the Queen and Prince Philip up close, but my French-Canadian friends were not interested. So, I went to the Chateau Frontenac, where the Queen was going to be received, with some student friends from the United States to watch the parade. And as the Queen and Prince drove by, we waved at them and they to us. But the zenith of the separatist demonstrations would be set by General Charles de Gaulle's visit to Montreal in the summer of 1967.

General De Gaulle, as Head of State, ignored protocol, which required all Heads of State to first visit Ottawa, the federal capital, and be officially received by the Governor General of Canada. Rather, General De Gaulle decided to do otherwise. He travelled on a French naval ship, Colbert, that first stopped in Quebec City where he was well received by the Prime Minister of Quebec, Daniel Johnson. Then he travelled down the Saint Lawrence River to Montreal where he was warmly received by the Mayor of Montreal, Jean Drapeau, Daniel Johnson, Prime Minister of Quebec, and a sea of jubilant Montrealers. It was during his address to the crowd that he uttered the controversial phrase, "Vive le Quebec Libre." ("Long Live Free Quebec"), with a deliberate emphasis on the word "Libre."

English Canadians were incensed by this gross diplomatic blunder. General De Gaulle had deliberately breached diplomatic protocol and had insulted the Canadian Government and its people. The proclamation produced an immediate reaction from Ottawa and across Canada. There was a flurry of radio commentaries and editorials in leading Canadian news media underscoring the role that Canada had played during the Second World War in the liberation of France and how dare General De Gaulle meddle in Canada's internal affairs! There were retaliatory statements by English Canadians such as "Vive Saint Pierre et Miquelon Libre" (two French possessions off the coast of southwest Newfoundland). The Prime Minister of Canada, Lester B Pearson, gave the General forty-eight hours to leave the country. Nevertheless, the damage had been done. General De Gaulle had endorsed the Quebec Separatist Movement. He had meddled in the situation of another country by taking sides. The flames of the hundred Years' war between Britain and France had been reignited. The battles at Hastings and Agincourt were alive again. Joan of Arc was on the move, and, on the Plains of Abraham, General Montcalm and General Wolfe were again fighting to conquer Quebec in honour of their respective nations.

It was rather uncanny for me as a Sierra Leonean, who had come from a British colony, to fathom such violent protests by whites against another white nation. I had been conditioned to view such political protests as being triggered by mainly black/white racial conflicts as had happened, for example, in Africa with European colonial powers or with the struggle for civil rights for African Americans in the United States. My understanding of this dynamic was shallow. Although a history major, I knew nothing of the Irish struggle for independence from the British, which lasted seven hundred years, and not much about the Russian Revolution. And the American and French Revolutions were events I had read about but not experienced. Yes, they had been violent but for me they were removed and not immediate as were the struggle for civil rights in the United States and black independence in Africa, which I had experienced and with which I could identify. However, as I grew older and became better informed and more worldly in my travels and understanding of human behaviour, I began to understand that such protests or conflicts were not necessarily rooted in white/black racism, but that it was rather human and nuanced; and where people felt oppressed, be it conflicts involving white against white, black against black or yellow against yellow, they would show their indignation by revolting.

I had arrived in Quebec City on a beautiful, cool, crisp, sunny, September morning having travelled all night on a train from Columbus, Ohio. I soon discovered that this was a picturesque and quaint city with lovely parks and historical sites that attracted a lot of tourists from the United States, English Canada, and beyond. The city was built overlooking the Saint Lawrence River, the Chateau Frontenac, and the City Ramparts, two famous historical landmarks, being located on strategic positions with a commanding view of the river and the town of Levis. The city comprised two parts, a lower and upper town, and an old and modern section. At the time of my arrival, the Faculty of Letters was in the old city on Rue Sainte Famille, but the following year it joined the new campus ("Cite Universitaire ") in Sainte Foy. I took a room in a house on Rue Saint Louis, which was within easy walking distance from my faculty. There was also another student from Sierra Leone by the name of Lahai Sogbandi who had also come to Quebec from the United States to pursue a master's degree in French. We became friends. He was married to a Sierra Leonean woman who prepared Sierra Leonean dishes to which I would be invited to partake.

My first winter in Canada was long, bitter, and arduous. It was very much unlike what I had experienced in Ohio. The university cafeteria was located at the main campus in Saint Foy. I had to buy my meals from restaurants in the touristic area of the city and was limited by my funds as to what I could eat. It was very much unlike my situation in the United States where I had had access to large quantities of food at the student cafeteria. I started losing weight and experienced sharp pains in my chest as the winter progressed. By the end of that first winter, I had lost over twenty pounds, prompting a friend to remark when I returned to the United States for a visit, "Don't they feed you in Canada?" I had to see one of the university doctors who told me that I had come down with the mumps following an analysis of my blood. He treated me, but I continued to feel the pains in my chest, and when I brought my situation again to his attention, he was not customer friendly. He told me to take an aspirin. I decided to see another doctor. I called on one whose office I passed by every day on my way to and from the university. He examined me and told me that I had an infection in my lungs, which he treated with penicillin, and the pains subsided. He later did a chest x-ray whose results were fine. When I asked him how much I owed, he replied, "nothing," adding that I was a student and that his daughter was also a student at L'Universite Laval. I was touched by his generosity and compassion. He also counselled me to take my shower in the evenings in the winter, rather than in the mornings. This advice proved to be very useful.

Becoming ill in Canada was unlike my experience in the United States where I had never been ill, other than for minor colds, during my four-year stay. Accordingly, I started to make sure that I ate well and when the summer came, I played soccer and tennis. This regime worked, as I never became ill during the remainder of my stay. The following year the Faculty of Letters moved to the main Campus in Saint Foy. I shared a three-bedroom apartment on Avenue Dallaire with two French-Canadian students. A year later I moved to Avenue Lienard, which was closer to the university, (a fifteen-minute walk). I shared a two-bedroom apartment with a Ghanaian student by the name of Hilary Ziniel who was pursuing a Masters' degree in the French Language Programme. The apartment was fully furnished, and we prepared our meals. On the completion of his degree, Hillary took an appointment with the Ghanaian Ministry of Foreign Affairs and served as a diplomat in Dakar, Senegal and New York, cities where I visited him.

I was admitted to the pre-masters' course, which had been established for English speakers. It comprised courses in Intensive French language and Grammar, Translation, (English to French), French Civilization, French Literature (Middle Ages to the Twentieth Century) Phonetics, Composition. Language and Grammar courses were given every day of the week, starting with lab sessions in the morning, and courses in Literature and Linguistics were held once a week. The system was more European than American where a course would meet three times a week. Grammar was intense and so were translations from English to French which required knowledge of the finer aspects of the French Language and grammar. To enter the master's programme all applicants had to pass a stiff exam requiring proficiency of French Grammar and Literature. Students had the option of finishing the master's programme either with thesis or without. Those students who opted for the non-thesis programme had to take three extra courses in addition to the curriculum for the thesis programme. Most of the students including me opted for the non-thesis programme. Professors whose courses were greatly esteemed were Jean Darbelnet's Stylistique Comparee (English and French). Professor Darbelnet demanded a lot from his students. If you handed in a paper in which you had made a stupid/careless grammatical mistake, you automatically received a zero regardless of the content of your work. He used to say in French, "you cannot afford to be making that type of grammatical mistake at the master's level." Accordingly, one made sure that one's paper had been proofread at least three times before submission. Other professors also esteemed were, Clement Moisan, Nineteenth Century French Literature (Flaubert, Stendhal, Lamartine, Hugo), Real Ouellette, Eighteenth Century French Literature, (Montesquieu, Voltaire, Rousseau, Diderot). I very much enjoyed 18th Century French writers, Voltaire and Montesquieu, whose analyses of French society attracted my curiosity, especially their ironic use of "the noble savage" as a narrative technique to critique society. 20th Century writers such as Albert Camus, Jean Paul Satre, André Malraux, and Antoine de Saint-Exupery were also stimulating. To highlight the achievement of mankind in the 20th century, Saint Exupery's humanistic novel, "Terre des Hommes" ("Man and his World'"), had served as the theme for Expo 67. Preparing for final exams at the end of the school year presented a strong challenge, this time a challenge between nature and the will to study.

After a long bitter winter, there would be beautiful sunny spring days of warm weather, which impacted on students—they wanted to be outdoors to take in the sun. Instead of studying, students would spend hours frolicking on the grass. Socially, I had a pleasant experience in Quebec. The only drawback was its harsh long winters which had prompted Gilles Vigneault, a popular French-Canadian folk singer and poet, to observe that his country was not a country, but rather it was winter. ("Mon pays ce n'est pas un pays, c'est l'hiver.") By three o'clock in the afternoon, it would be pitch black and this situation lasted for four months. There were also lots of Foreign Students: Africans, Asians, Europeans, Latin-Americans, Americans and West Indians, and this mixture made for a lively environment at the university where dances were held on Friday evenings at the Campus Centre in Sainte Foy. I remember an incident that occurred on my first day at the university that foreshadowed my positive racial experience in Canada. It had been raining and I had just entered the building and was waiting with other students for registration instructions. While I waited, a female student came up to me, her hair wet from the rain, and asked whether I had a comb that she could use as she wanted to fix her hair. I replied "no." She thanked me and walked away. I was taken aback by the innocence of her request, asking me, a black man, for a comb as she was white, and we were complete strangers. I never did experience overt racism in Canada. I do not recall my French or English Canadian classmates asking the types of questions that I had been subjected to while I was at Otterbein or maybe I had become less sensitive to those types of questions due to my experience in the United States. But this does not mean that Canadians do not harbour ill feelings against non-whites. Lawrence

Hill's novel, *Book of Negroes*[20], and Kevin Lowther's novel, *The Odyssey of John Kizell*[21], amply describe the trials and tribulations of African Americans who emigrated, after the American Revolution, from the United States to Nova Scotia, a Province often referred to by Black Canadians as the "Mississippi of the North."

Nevertheless, an incident did occur that made me question my relationship with the church and religion in general. It happened at the Anglican cathedral in Quebec City. As an Anglican, who was raised in Sierra Leone and had been confirmed before leaving Sierra Leone for my studies abroad, I was pleased to have found an Anglican church where I could worship, whose liturgy I was familiar with, and which was within easy walking distance from my residence. I used to attend services on a regular basis although this had not been the case when I was in Ohio, as I did not feel comfortable at some of the churches that I attended. I informed the Dean of the Cathedral that I was a student from Sierra Leone attending L'Universite Laval. The Dean welcomed me, and I felt accepted. I related my experiences to two white American student friends of mine, who were not Anglican, and invited them to attend services with me. I introduced them to the Dean who also welcomed them, and the three of us made it a practice of attending Sunday services together. One day my friends informed me that they had been invited on several occasions to tea parties at the residence of the Dean who introduced them to his family and members of the Anglican community in Quebec City. My friends wanted to know why I was not present at the parties. I responded that I had not been invited. My friends expressed surprise that I had not been invited, and disappointment at the behaviour of the Dean especially as I was responsible for introducing them to the church. I was

---

[20] . Lawrence Hill, "The Book of Negroes", Harper Collins, Canada, 2007.
[21] . Kevin Lowther,G., "Odyssey of John Kizell," Columbia, South Carolina, University of South Carolina Press, 2011.

disheartened to discover what had happened and felt rejected or disparaged because of my colour. I surmised that as a black person, it was permissible to be seen in church but not good enough to be invited home. I decided to stop going to the church - a decision that would later have a profound impact on my spirituality. The incident was a defining moment in my struggle to understand the complexities of human behaviour. I felt people were hypocrites, dishonest in their comportment, and that some use religion as a front to cover up their own prejudices, be it racial or otherwise. Those who had taken a vow to improve human relationship through religion were regretfully its saboteurs. Based on my religious experiences in the United States and this incident in Canada, I became cynical towards the church and religion in general.

There were also lots of home parties and dinners organised by students, and such occasions produced very lively discussions on politics, economics, literature, music and the arts and sports (hockey). The question of a Canadian identity was always a sore spot that triggered passionate reactions. Canadians would become incensed by careless remarks made by Americans regarding their identity. Americans often noted that Canadians were a people in search of an identity, as they would define themselves as not being American but not who they were. Canadians would respond by referring to the salad as a metaphor for nationhood. They would use the metaphor to explain who they were. "We are like a salad. For the salad to exist, it must be whole, but the salad is composed of its different separate entities that are identifiable. We are proud of these different entities. We are not like you Americans who are a melting pot where all identities become lost in becoming an American." It appeared to me that our French-Canadian friends seemed better prepared to define their "Canadianess" because of their French language culture than their English Canadian brethren. I used to say to myself that Americans and Canadians were like first cousins having a family feud. Each party loved the other dearly but, alas, sometimes, could not stand the other. However, it would not be wrong for me to observe that American cultural influence in Canada was very strong, and despite the excellent programmes of the Canadian Broadcasting Corporation, such as the talk shows, "This Hour has Seven Days," "Sunday," the pervasiveness of American television programmes was significant.

In addition to events organised by the International Students Committee there was an African Students Union that also organised social events such as celebrating Independence Day Anniversaries of African nations. The Universal Declaration of Independence by the Ian Smith government of Rhodesia in November of 1965 brought together African and non-African students to demonstrate against this illegal regime. Students gathered in front of the British High Commissioner's office in Quebec City with placards denouncing the illegal white supremacist regime of Ian Smith. There was international condemnation of the Smith regime that caused Britain and its Commonwealth members as well as the United Nations to impose economic sanctions on the illegal government of Rhodesia. Despite the international isolation, Rhodesia continued to exist with the support of the white government of South Africa and the colonial government of Portugal. Two other events that impacted African students were the overthrow of Kwame Nkrumah, the President of Ghana, and the assassination of Hendrik Verwoerd, Prime Minister of South Africa, and the architect of apartheid. Both incidents happened in 1966, Nkrumah was overthrown in February and Verwoerd was assassinated in September. The reaction among the Ghanaian students was mixed. There were those who deeply regretted the event and others whose reactions ranged from being nonchalant to celebratory. Most of the non-Ghanaian African students sided with those Ghanaians who regretted the incident and saw Nkrumah's overthrow as a major setback to African nationalism as its leading spokesman was no more. However, Verwoerd assassination was greeted with jubilation. Some African students, donned in their traditional dress, went to the cafeteria to celebrate, thanking providence for taking the life of Verwoerd this time, as he had survived an assignation attempt some five years earlier.

Our apartment neighbour, a middle-aged French-Canadian woman, used to take pity on Hillary and me by giving us lovely French-Canadian dishes and desserts that she had prepared. She was very motherly to us and would observe that we were struggling students who did not eat good homemade food. One day she gave us a bottle of South African wine, noting that she had been shopping and had seen the wine. She decided to present us the wine as a remembrance of "our country." We accepted the wine and thanked her for her kindness; but never drank it. However, another African student friend, who visited us regularly and was "less political" than us, had noticed that the wine had been on the dining room table for a long time untouched. He wondered why it had not been used. We told him that the wine, a gift from our neighbour, was from South Africa and we were not going to condone apartheid by drinking it. He said he was against apartheid but had no problems with South African wines. He finished the bottle of wine, observing with a smack of his lips followed by a large burp that "good things should not be wasted."

Quebec summers and history attracted tourists from all over the world including naval ships whose sailors would be grabbed by young "Quebecoise." Having a summer cabin as a relaxation escape point from the hectic life of a metropolis was a common Canadian tradition. Foreign students got invited by their Canadian friends to these cabins where we had fun fishing, cooking/grilling, dining, and washing down our meals with fine wines. I became friends with an American female music student from Maine and together we attended social events, classical concerts and, on weekends, explored the beautiful autumn countryside of Quebec in her car. We often drove to Isle d'Orleans, where we would eat at a quaint restaurant called L'Artre, visited Montmorency Falls, Sainte Anne de

Beaupre, a favourite pilgrimage point, and the town of Chicoutimi.

During the summer, I played soccer on a team called "Cosmopolite" organised by a group of Guinean Students led by Paul Baruxakis who was the captain. I had not played the game since I left Sierra Leone in 1959 and had taken up smoking. I had to rework myself into shape. The team comprised players from Africa, Latin-America, and Europe. I would later meet Paul in Conakry when I worked for an international organisation in the late nineties. It so happened that he had family ties in Freetown whom I knew. Paul showed me photographs of our soccer team. Both of us had aged during the intervening years. The following autumn and summer I played on Universite Laval soccer team coached by Georges Ambassa, a student from Cameroon. The team was composed of African and Caribbean players.

My sporting experiences in Quebec cannot end without describing my attempt at skiing. A student friend who was an excellent skier invited me to the skiing lodge at Lac Beauport. It was a beautiful sunny afternoon and lots of people were out skiing. He took me to the gentler slopes and told me to practice there. But after a while it was no fun, and I decided to venture to a steeper slope. I made it halfway up the slope in one of these machines that went between your legs and pulled you up the hill. Then I panicked when I saw the distance to which I had to descend. There was no way I could descend that slope on skis. Accordingly, I had to fall on my buttocks several times to descend. Onlookers were cracking up with laughter, while I shouted for help. That day I thought I would die. I never attempted the sport again, although I went tobogganing with friends several times.

A favourite winter activity was the Winter Carnival of Quebec City. I'm told it is the only winter carnival in the western hemisphere. The carnival precedes Lent. For three weeks the streets of Quebec are filled with carnival-jubilation folks, dancing and having a great time drinking from their special walking sticks into which various forms of alcohol had been poured. The winters were so cold that my beard would freeze during a short walk, for example the fifteen-minute walk from my apartment on Avenue Lienard to the Faculty of Human Sciences (later named Pavillon de Konnick) is a case in point. The symbol of the carnival was the "bon homme" whose majestic ice palace, built with ice blocks, would last for four to six weeks before slowly disappearing as the temperature warmed up. There were also many outdoor activities such as hockey games and men racing across the ice-jammed Saint Lawrence River on boats. The climax of the carnival was the parade that led to the crowning of the Queen in bitter cold weather.

Expo 67, the World's Fair, was hosted by Canada in the city of Montreal. The event was a massive success as tourists came from all over the world to behold this spectacle. I had bought a season ticket the year before at a very good price, which gave me unlimited access, and I was able to visit the fair on several occasions with friends. One such person was John Moorhead, my college roommate at Otterbein, who was living in New York City. After visiting me in Quebec, we took the train down to Montreal and visited the fair. Montreal was a good escape point for students. It was a more cosmopolitan city than Quebec with superior social amenities, such as museums, classical concerts, discos, bistros, good ethnic and French cuisines, etc. It was a pleasure to visit the city, which I considered my favourite in North America. It had a beautiful metro system with spectacular underground shopping centres at Place Ville Marie and Place Bonaventure. If one became tired of Montreal, there was always Boston and New York City. Sierra Leonean friends that visited while I was in Quebec were Dr. Oju Mends and his wife, Yeni. Dr. Mends conducted research in Pathology at McGill University, Rogers Jones, a student at Ottawa, Freddy Noah, a student at Catholic University in Washington DC and a former roommate at Otterbein, Nqobisizwe Akintunde Adekayode (formerly, Richard Gordon Harris), a student at Dalhousie, in Nova Scotia with whom I had attended primary and secondary schools in Sierra Leone.

Close student friends of the era were: Yves Albert. He introduced me to his family who gave me an open invitation to their home. Indeed, I had the key to their house and could come and go at my discretion. Yves became a folklore singer and was very popular in the Quebec folkloric scene in the sixties and seventies. Unfortunately, I have lost touch with him. Benjamin Kumpwo, a homeboy of my roommate, Hilary Ziniel, from Ghana, completed a master's degree in French. Benjamin would later take up a teaching assignment at the University of Sciences and Technology where he taught French. Yvette Balkie Kamara, a Sierra Leonean student completed a master's degree in French. She would later take up an appointment at Harford School for Girls, in Moyamba, Sierra Leone. Her older brother, Alex Kamara, and I had attended the Prince of Wales and played cricket on the school's team. Maka Diallo, younger brother of Diallo Telli, the first Secretary General of the Organisation of African Unity who was imprisoned at Camp Boiro,[22] in Conakry, Guinea by Sekou Toure, President of Guinea, and died from starvation and torture, and was buried in an unmarked grave. I had the honour of meeting this well-respected African statesman in Quebec when he visited his younger brother, Maka, in 1965. Maka completed a Ph.D. in Economics. I also met Diallo Telli's wife when I lived in Conakry in the late nineties. Ousmane Diop was a Mathematics and Statistics Professor from Guinea at L'Universite Laval. He was also imprisoned in Camp Boiro in Conakry, Guinea, but was released. He had returned home to serve his country when the arrest happened. I would later meet him in Guinea, and we were able to renew our friendship. Richard Campion, an American student from New Jersey who invited me to his

---

[22] . A prison in Conakry, Guinea were political opponents of President Ahmed Sekou Toure were imprisoned, tortured and/or starved to death.

home where I met his family. He married a Canadian woman and they stayed in Canada. Michel de Courval, a French-Canadian student who also introduced me to his family and was the life of our parties, and Jagan Senghore and Crispin Grey-Johnson, both from the Gambia with relatives in Sierra Leone. They were students at McGill University in Montreal and attended French Summer School at Universite Laval.

Chapter: 12

Greensboro - A Major Turning Point in my Academic Life

In the autumn of 1967, I accepted a position to teach French at North Carolina Agricultural and Technical State University (commonly referred to as North Carolina A&T or A&T) in Greensboro, North Carolina. I already had a connection with the university through my father, who had taught there from 1926 to 1928 and had been a Fulbright Professor from 1959-61. Several students from Sierra Leone and other African countries had studied at North Carolina A&T, especially in Agriculture and Education. One such student was Mr. Musa (Moses) Kamara who had completed both his undergraduate and graduate degrees at A&T and had been offered a teaching and administrative position at the university. He and I bonded and became fast friends. I would later be his best man when he married Barbara Sia Fergusson of Wilmington, North Carolina, who had served as a Peace Corps Volunteer in Liberia. She introduced me to my godmother, Carrie Guerphan Hargrave, also of Wilmington, North Carolina, who had spent three years (in the late thirties and early forties) in Sierra Leone as a Missionary.

Living in North Carolina was my first experience in the American South and life there was unlike my student days in Ohio and the contrast even more acute when compared to my days in Quebec. In Ohio as well as in other states of the Midwest and the South, not all public facilities (e.g., restaurants, movie theatres, hotels/motels, tennis, and golf clubs, swimming pools, drinking fountains, toilets,) were integrated in the early sixties. This was unlike my experience in Quebec where I did not experience any overt discrimination, hostile reaction, or the refusal of service, not even in a barbershop. I remember an incident in Quebec when I went to a barbershop for a haircut and the barber told me that he had never cut a black man's hair but that he was willing to try. His excuse sounded like an apology for not having had the opportunity to cut a black man's hair. With my supervision, he gingerly cut my hair, and the product was fine. This incident was very much unlike my experience in Westerville, Ohio, where the barber asked me what I wanted when I entered his shop. I thought it was a funny question, so I politely said, "a haircut." He sat me down and proceeded to scalp my head. He took the shares and went from the front of the head to the back, until my entire head was completely bald. I never went back. Each time I needed a haircut after that experience, I would go to a black barber in Columbus. I would plan the haircut together with other shopping activities that I had to do in Columbus to capitalise on my meagre funds. As an African in North Carolina, I felt honoured to be teaching at one of America's finest black institutions that had played and continues to play a significant role in the struggle for civil rights for African Americans. North Carolina A&T was famous in that it had kick-started the lunch-counter demonstrations to integrate public eating facilities in the South in the early sixties, which further triggered the Freedom Rides. A famous civil rights leader in the person of the Reverend Jesse Jackson, a principal aide of the valiant Civil rights leader, Dr. Martin Luther King, was a graduate of North Carolina A&T and his legacy was very much alive when I arrived in Greensboro in 1967. Teaching at A&T also offered me the opportunity to experience the sufferings of African Americans through its magnificent choir. Witnessing the choir perform Negro Spirituals and the African American national anthem ("Lift Every Voice and Sing" by James Weldon Johnson) was an emotional experience that brought tears to my eyes or gave me goose pimples.

The focus of my department was to provide language courses in (French, Spanish, and German), to students who were fulfilling the university core requirements for graduation. It was mainly a service department although there were a handful of students who majored in French but not so for Spanish and German. I was responsible for teaching principally first- and second-year French Language courses and I interacted well with my students. Nevertheless, teaching was not without its challenges. This was my first teaching experience and there was a lot to learn. For example, at the time of a midterm or final exam or quiz, students had the habit of fabricating excuses to avoid taking the test or dispensing a lot of energy searching wastepaper baskets for stencil copies of discarded exam questions. Students knew I was new, young, and not much older than some of them. At the end of the first semester of my teaching, I developed guidelines for addressing these negative behaviours. Henceforth, at the beginning of a new term I would discuss these guidelines to make sure they understood my expectations and their responsibilities. I would also do the same at mid-term to reinforce each other's responsibilities once again. This strategy worked. It ended the excuses. I also learned that I had to be vigilant when monitoring tests. During a regular class session, I recall asking a student (male) a simple question which should have posed no problem to him as he was an "A student". He had scored A's on the two tests that had been done so far. I was surprised when he could not answer the question. Accordingly, the next time I gave a test, I separated his neighbour (a female student) from him, and he failed miserably. I emphasise gender here only to note that the female students in general did very much better than their male counterparts who had other responsibilities as well as other social distractions. But there were male students who excelled and were leaders in the making. Approximately twenty-two years later, when I was working with USAID in Nigeria, I met a former student who was with the military at the American Embassy in Lagos. We met at a social gathering at the Ambassador's residence. He came up and introduced himself by asking me, "Sir, have you lived in North Carolina?" to which I responded, "yes." He then asked, "did you teach French at North Carolina A&T?" I said "yes," and he responded, "I was your student. My name is Spencer." I looked at him and said, "Indeed, I do remember you." He was now a Full Colonel in the US Army serving as the Chief Military Attaché at the Embassy.

Living in Greensboro and teaching at A&T was also a period of substantial educational and intellectual growth for me, making the experience **a major turning point in my life.** This was the late sixties, a period of intense social and political unrest in America, attributed to the war in Viet Nam and the struggle for civil rights. There had been very popular youth protests against the war at such major universities as Columbia, the University of California at Berkeley, the University of Wisconsin at Madison, and at Cornell. A few years earlier, most African nations had become independent from their European colonial masters and this change has impacted positively on African Americans, especially on such civil rights leaders as Malcolm X and Kwame Toure (Stokely Carmichael). In Washington D.C the African American elite formed, for example, social groups such as "Friends of Ghana," "Friends of Nigeria," and "Friends of Sierra Leone," etc. These groups provided social avenues for African Americans to get to know Africans and vice-versa. African American students were also leading protests in America's top universities such as Harvard and Cornell for the establishment of Black Studies, which comprised African American, African, and Caribbean studies. There had been riots following the assassinations of the Civil Rights leader, Dr. Martin Luther King, and the popular Senator, Robert Kennedy of New York. Some of these riots took place on A&T's campus and the State Governor sent in the national guards to quell the uprisings. One student was killed, shot to death in his dormitory by a national guard. His death sparked off more rioting. The university was closed until order was restored. There was the cry for Black Power in the speeches of Stokely Carmichael (Kwame Toure and H. Rap Brown). I had met Stokely Carmichael on two occasions when he gave speeches at A&T. As fate would have it, I attended his funeral and witnessed his burial in Conakry, Guinea, in 1998, during my tour with USAID in that country. Despite racism, I also discovered that the black middle class lived better in the South compared to their brethren in the North.

There was also cultural affirmation of blackness in such popular expressions as "Black is Beautiful", "I'm Black and Proud" as well as in the lyrics of songs performed by such artists as James Brown, Aretha Franklin, and Nina Simone. There were cultural manifestations such as the Afro haircut and the donning of dashiki shirts and the bubu and lappa (wrapper). There was the call for studying African languages such as Ki-Swahili, Hausa, Yoruba, etc. I recall going to social gatherings in Washington D.C. and black women would be dressed in African attire, and it was only their accents that betrayed their American identity. There was the creation of the Afro-American Heritage Society, in Montreal, in 1969, by African American Scholars as a protest to the African Studies Association which, they felt, was dominated by white scholars. It was during this period that I also started to question my education and my identity. Although I was African, born and bred on the African continent, other than my blackness, my intellectual reference, starting with my schooling in Sierra Leone and my university education in the United States and Canada, had been essentially European cantered. For example, Sierra Leone had been "discovered" by a Portuguese explorer (Pedro da Cintra) in 1462 and that he named the area Sierra Leoa because of the topography which looked like a lion to him, and the lighting and thunder sounded like roaring lions. Europeans had come to the West African coast, since the early 14th century, to buy enslaved Africans from African chiefs. Sierra Leone was founded in 1787 with the settlement of the Black Poor from England supported by English abolitionists. Sierra Leone became a crown colony under British domination in 1808. In 1925, His Royal Highness, the Prince of Wales, visited Sierra

Leone and founded my secondary school which he named, "the Prince of Wales." As a result of this awareness, I decided to use my African name "Modupe" (meaning "gratitude" in the Yoruba language) instead of Sylvester and to replace Sylvester with "Sundiata," the name of the great 17th century leader of Mali. Much later after taking the Ancestry DNA Test, I would discover that 5% of my ethnicity was from Mali. My academic awareness was further awakened when I happened on a book in A&T's library written by a Belgian scholar.[23] The book focused on the writings of three primary black writers who created the Negritude Movement: one African (Leopold Sedar Senghor from Senegal whom I had the honour of meeting while a student at l'Universite Laval when he visited Quebec city in 1965 and gave a lecture on Francophonie, at the university) and the other two Caribbean (Aime Cesaire, from Martinique, and Leon Damas from the former French Guiana). The Negritude philosophy would lay the foundation for African nationalism in the French African countries, and Leopold Sedar Senghor would become the first President of Senegal. The experience derived from reading this book was bittersweet. Bitter, in that I had spent my entire life without any knowledge of these writers. Sweet in the discovery of these writings whose themes I could identify with. Indeed, my studies of French Literature at Otterbein and Laval Universities had not exposed me to Black writers from Africa or the Caribbean. Consequently, I decided to immerse myself in reading works of Black writers from Africa, the United States, and the Caribbean. I read Chancellor Williams' "The Destruction of Black Civilization", Carter G. Woodson's "The Mis-Education of the Negro", Richard Wright, "Blackboy", "The Outsider", Leopold Senghor's "Snow Upon Paris", "Black Woman", Chinua Achebe's "Things Fall Apart", Mongo Beti's

---

[23]. Lilyan Kesteloot, "Les écrivains noirs de la langue française-naissance d'une littérature, Bruxelles, Editions de l'Institut de Sociologie, 1963.

"Mission Accomplished", William Conton's "The African" and Lenrie Peters' "The Second Round".[24] I also read about the Harlem Renaissance and benefitted from the knowledge of two pundits on African-American Literature in A&T's English Department: Dr. Darwin Turner and Dr. Walter Daniel. Through these readings I became a "resource person" on African literature and my colleagues would request me to discuss writers such as Chinua Achebe and Wole Soyinka with their students. I also took part in cultural sessions where I would read and discuss poems such as, "Black Woman" by Senghor or "Hiccups" by Leon Damas. The discovery of African, African American and Caribbean literature ignited the flame in me to further my studies in this area. Two colleagues at A&T, who had taken graduate degrees at the University of Wisconsin-Madison in History and Political Science respectively, informed me of the African Studies Programme at the University of Wisconsin-Madison, and the existence of the Department of African Languages and Literature. This news was a godsend. It was exactly the type of Department I was in search of. I also had the good fortune of meeting one of the African Professors of the Department (Dr. Edris Makward from Senegal and the Gambia,) who had been invited to give a lecture on "Negritude" at A&T. I informed him of my interests, and he would later serve as my advisor when I embarked on a Ph.D. programme at Wisconsin. He told me that African languages such as Ki-Swahili, Hausa, "Arabic", and Xhosa, were being taught in the Department. This information further spiced my appetite.

Intellectually, I, along with other junior professors, interacted more with students than we did with the senior professors at the university. We, the junior professors, were closer in age with students and identified with their concerns. Furthermore, we were also not married and thus did not have family responsibilities as our senior colleagues. Nevertheless,

---

[24]. Lenrie Peters happens to be my cousin on the Broderick side of my family, See P. 11 above.

the students' quest for more intellectual stimulation continued, and when they found a professor who was knowledgeable; they seized the opportunity to tap his/her intellectual resources. Accordingly, we, junior professors (black and white), responded by promoting discussion groups on the writings of such authors as Frantz Fanon, Leopold Senghor, Julius Nyerere, Kwame Nkrumah, Malcolm X, Eldridge Cleaver. The students were more interested in matters African American and African in addition to the subject matter of their traditional curriculum. This interest corresponded with mine, and I was able to combine some of my teachings and research findings with those of colleagues in the Departments of History, Political Science and English. Speakers such as Stokely Carmichael, James Turner of the African Studies Programme at Cornell University, Edris Makward from the African Studies Programme at Wisconsin were invited to give lectures. I befriended French Professors at the University of North Carolina at Greensboro and invited a few to give lectures on various topics on French Literature and Language. To conclude one could say there was agitation on the part of the students for more Black Studies including languages, but the university administration was not able to yield to their demands as Black Studies programmes were still in their infancy and only a few universities had developed a viable methodology for their implementation. Furthermore, the university was not psychologically ready for this transformation.

Another area that benefitted me while at A&T was to serve as a VISTA Volunteer (Volunteers in Service to America), the domestic equivalent of the Peace Corps. A colleague was managing the VISTA programme, and it was designed to promote Consumer Education in the poor white and black neighbourhoods in the city of Greensboro, North Carolina. The programme comprised some twenty volunteers both whites and blacks. Whites worked in poor white communities and blacks in poor black communities. Following our training, we started working in our respective communities and met every evening as a group to take stock of the day's activities and to strategize for the following day's work. Primarily, we were tasked to inform poor citizens of ways they could save their precious funds by shopping in large supermarkets where they could get fresh products, better food choices, and where the prices were more competitive compared to the exorbitant prices in neighbourhood stores, notwithstanding the poor quality of the food products. Shopping in such stores afforded customers the opportunity to develop a relationship with store owners and thus could obtain credit, or cash their social security and or pay checks. To address the issue of distance, we took groups out shopping in our cars or counselled them to go in groups in a taxi and share the taxi fare. The target groups listened to our recommendations but did not change their behaviours as they were pretty set in their ways. Personal resentment against members of the programme was directed against the manager who was white and had moderate long hair. One day on a monitoring visit of a volunteer in a poor white community, an angry white man with a shotgun chased him. The aggressor could not tolerate a white male with long hair. For him all white men with long hair were hippies, social misfits, and easy game for physical attacks. My manager had to take to his heels, leaving his car behind, which was later retrieved by the volunteer whom he had gone to monitor. At the conclusion of the programme, the consensus was that the volunteers had benefited more from the programme's marketing and consumer strategies than we had been able to give to the members of our target groups.

In August of 1970, I ended my tenure with A&T and left for Madison, Wisconsin, to start a Ph.D. in African Literature. The decision to leave A&T was not easy as I had carved a niche in my department and made a lot of friends with faculty members and students. When I broached the subject with my Department Head, he was not pleased. He told me that he was grooming me for taking over the Department chairmanship from him when he retired. I thanked him for his confidence and faith in me but that my mind was made up. I told him that once I completed my studies, I could always return to A&T. I also discussed the matter with my good friend and older brother, Musa Kamara, who gave me his support. Later he and I would meet in Madison when he would come up on work visits. He headed a programme at A&T that sent students to the University of Wisconsin-Madison for a semester.

I was also offered a position to teach French at Lincoln University in Missouri by Dr. Walter Daniel of the English Department at North Carolina A&T. Dr. Daniel, a mentor of mine, had been appointed President of Lincoln University, and was moving shortly to Missouri. Attractive as the offer was, I informed Dr. Daniel that I had already made plans to start work on my Ph.D. studies at the University of Wisconsin at Madison and respectfully declined his offer. We agreed to stay in touch. While I was at Wisconsin, I shared with Dr. Daniel some of my early publications.

Chapter: 13

"On Wisconsin"[25]

I drove from Greensboro, North Carolina, to Madison, Wisconsin, one of America's finest college towns, spending the night in Worthington, Ohio with Helen, and Howard Ware whom I had met while I was at Otterbein University in the early sixties. They had hosted our graduation party and had introduced us to African American students from Columbus, Ohio. My sojourn at Madison, educationally and socially, was very unlike what I had experienced anywhere else. It was intense, stimulating, political and racial. When I got to Madison I was "greeted" with the bombing of the University of Wisconsin's Army Math Research Center in Sterling Hall from which a student had been killed and the perpetuators of the bombing were on the run. There were demonstrations on campus against the Vietnam War and on several occasions the police had to disperse the crowds with tear gas on campus and on State Street, the main thoroughfare between the university and the State Capital Building. On several occasions there would be policemen in classrooms observing Professors' discussions. I recall being in the Graduate Reading Room at the Memorial Library when a policeman came in and took a student away.

Considering the killings at the Sikh Temple, Oak Creek, Wisconsin, I must mention that there were two racially-motivated deaths during my stay in Madison. The city of Madison was a bastion of liberalism and counterculture, especially in the districts adjacent to the university, and "Madisonians" were proud of their city and its progressive culture. The first killing took place, my second year, in a private residence hall on Frances Street, where a black

---

[25] . Fight song of the University of Wisconsin Badgers and of the State of Wisconsin.

student was killed by an angry white man in a building that I had lived in the year before. It was reported that the perpetrator became aggravated by his daughter, who was dating a black student. The perpetrator went to the floor where he thought the student lived and shot and killed the first black student that appeared. It turned out that the student he shot was not the person dating his daughter. The perpetrator was arrested and judged not well in the head. The second incident occurred a few months before I departed Madison.

An interracial couple had gone to the East Town Mall and when they returned to their car, they were gunned down by a sniper, who escaped. Sixteen years later, on a visit to Madison I enquired whether the culprit (s) had ever been apprehended. I was told no. [26]

Other than these disturbances, I found the academic experience at the University of Wisconsin- Madison, intellectually challenging, inspirational, and sound. I enjoyed very much the intellectual and social rapport that we had with our professors whom we called by their first names and referred to them as Mister so and so and not Dr. or Professor So and So outside of academia, there were a lot of cultural events to spice our appetites. There were dance troops from several African countries that performed, there were plays galore to see, performances by distinguished American artists, and the showing of films on every night of the week—some first rate and others not.

"Controversial" political figures such as Angela Davis, Stokely Carmichael, and "non-controversial" such as Senator Muskie, to name but a few, were invited to give lectures. The students were receptive to the first two speakers. Unfortunately, the fate of Senator Musky would be different. He was unable to give his speech as he was prevented from doing so. Each time he started to talk, students heckled him by yelling, "LSD for Musky". In the end he gave up.

---

[26]. I do not know whether the culprit was ever apprehended.

The African Studies Programme, one of the strongest in the United States, was renowned for its interdisciplinary emphasis, which promoted cross fertilisation and added breadth and depth to one's intellectual development in and out of one's subject matter. The Programme comprised departments in Education, History, Political Science, Sociology, Agriculture, Agricultural Economics, Anthropology, Development, Geography, and Literature and Languages. The Programme only gave out a certificate on the completion of several required courses. Masters and Ph.D. degrees were offered by the relevant departments. I was very impressed with my professors' knowledge of their subjects. Some of them were internationally renowned and had published extensively. The library was also exceptional with a huge collection of materials on Africa. I spent hours in the library reading about Sierra Leone and wondering how little Sierra Leoneans knew about their country. The Programme usually had a social event in the autumn to welcome new students and introduce professors as well as in the spring, to close out the academic year. There were also private parties organised by professors or students, and on State Street, there were a variety of ethnic and American restaurants and taverns to frequent. The Department of African Languages and Literature (now renamed the Department of African Cultural Studies,) also had a social gathering at Christmas as well as in the spring. The famous "Mifflin Street Block Party" would take place in the Spring. The street would be blocked off and undergraduate students for the most part would party continuously for a weekend consuming kegs and kegs of beer. Beer was also available on a regular basis at the Student Union of which there were two: Memorial Union and Union South. The heavy party scene at Madison during the Fall, Spring and Summer earned the school the reputation of being continually voted the Number One-Party School in America. To say that students had fun at these extracurricular events would be an understatement. In addition to these social outlets, there were also a lot of foreign students from every continent of the world, and a large number were African from the length and breadth of the continent. As to be expected, the Nigerians formed the largest group. There was also the Madison area Committee on Southern Africa (MACSA) a community-based organisation including students and professors from the University. Among its multi goals were the provision of support for sanctions on minority regimes in Southern Africa and the provision of assistance to liberation movements, and the conducting of teach-ins and the holding of seminars to create awareness that resulted in the University of Wisconsin's decision to divest its investments in Southern African corporations.[27]

Weekends provided opportunities to drive to touristic sites such as Wisconsin Dells, Frank Lloyd Wright's buildings and Amish communities. Other nearby escape points were Milwaukee, Chicago, Minneapolis, and Door County in the fall. I had gone to the University of Wisconsin-Madison to study principally Modern African Literature both of English and French expressions in the Department of African Languages and Literature, the only department of its kind in the United States of America. But I soon discovered that there was another area in Africa that was being taught that fascinated me, namely, African Oral Narrative Traditions. Professor Jan Vansina of the History Department had been the leading scholar in this regard and would later contribute valuable information to Alex Haley on the origins of Kunta Kinte for his historical novel "Roots." Another specialist on oral traditions was Professor A C Jordan, from South Africa, who taught Southern African Oral Traditions in the Department of African Languages and Literature. Unfortunately, Professor Jordan had died by the time I arrived in Madison, but one of his students, Harold Scheub, had undertaken research in Southern Africa on the oral narrative traditions of the

---

[27]. "Madison Area Committee on Southern Africa-African Activist," accessed September 15, 2013, http://africanactivist,mau.edu/organization.php?name=Madison+Area+Committee+on+Southern+Africa.

Xhosa, Zulu and Ndebele. Following completion of his Ph.D., Scheub was hired on a full-time basis in the Department of African Languages and Literature. Professor Daniel Kunene, also a specialist on Southern African Literatures both oral and written, would join him. Other specialists in African Oral Traditions were Professor Neil Skinner who taught courses on Hausa and its oral traditions and Professor Philip Noss who taught a course on Gbaya (a Cameroonian Language) as well as a course on "Introduction to African Linguistics." In addition to my courses in Modern African Literature both English and French, taught by Edris Makward, I took extensive courses on Oral Narrative Traditions and Oral Societies; and decided I wanted to specialise in the Krio Oral Narrative Tradition of Sierra Leone. To prepare me for this exercise, I took courses in Linguistics, Literary Theory, Anthropology, and Oral Societies and their Narrative Traditions. For me the most stimulating courses were those on literary theory and criticism that employed both linguistic and literary models to analyse a work of art, both oral and written. I read widely on Russian Formalism, Semiotics, Structuralism, Post Structuralism, the works of Vladimir Propp, Roman Jakobsen, Claude Levi-Strauss, Roland Barthes, Suzanne Langer, Albert Lord, Mary Douglas, etc., and attended lectures/seminars given by Harold Scheub, Jan Vansina and Steven Feierman, scholars who emphasised critical methodological approaches for investigating oral societies. I also studied other African Languages such as Ki-Swahili under the tutelage of Lyndon Harries, a Ki-Swahili Specialist, formerly of the School of Oriental and African Studies (SOAS) of the University of London and Patrick Bennett, a graduate of SOAS and a specialist in Bantu Languages. Linguistics became my Ph.D. minor. I took courses on Krio language from Professor Jack Berry of Northwestern University, formerly of SOAS, as I had to demonstrate linguistic knowledge of this language, my major African language, to be admitted as a candidate for the Ph.D. degree. My department decided for me to go to Northwestern University to take a course from Professor Berry, a scholar on Sierra Leone Krio. Each week on a Friday I would undertake the two- and half-hour drive from Madison to Evanston, Illinois, to have classes with Professor Berry. Sometimes I spent the night and returned to Madison the following day. In addition to my academic studies, I was also a co-editor of the Department's Journal, Ba Shiru that was published twice a year. In the summer of 1972, I also took a six-week course on Mende, the largest linguistic group of Sierra Leone. After three years of course work and the passing of my Preliminary Examinations, I was admitted as a candidate for the Doctor of Philosophy Degree.

I was a recipient of a Wisconsin Ford Foundation Fellowship that also provided funding for my field research in Sierra Leone. I spent twelve months, September 1973-to September 1974, focusing on Krio Oral Narrative Traditions. I obtained affiliation as a Visiting Researcher with the African Studies Programme at Fourah Bay College, under the chairmanship of John Peterson who had undertaken research on the founding of Krio society in his seminal work, "The Province of Freedom." I was provided with an office and access to its Library. With a tape recorder I collected oral narratives from all the main Krio villages on the Sierra Leone peninsular, principally from native Krio speakers and secondarily from non-native speakers, as I wanted to identify Krio narrative images and patterns from non-Krio images and patterns, if they existed. Besides collecting narratives from the Sierra Leone peninsular, I collected narratives from other areas of Sierra Leone in Krio: Bonthe, Port Loko, Makeni, Kenema and Pujehun. Another colleague of mine from the University of Wisconsin-Madison, Donald Cosentino, was doing a similar study on Mende in a village outside of Bo. Also undertaking linguistic research on Krio was Wayne Williams (now Selassie Williams) from the University of Indiana, Department of Linguistics. Being back in Sierra Leone for a year gave me the opportunity to renew my contacts with family and relatives as well as with former schoolmates. My friend Nicholas Palmer had become a successful Pharmacist and was the proud owner of two Pharmacies. He would take me out to nightclubs and would insist that he had to pay because I was still a poor suffering student pursuing my studies.[28] Following the completion of my field research I was offered a temporary teaching position in the Department of African Languages and Literature, where I taught courses on African Oral Traditions and Modern African Literature. Teaching provided me with the opportunity to explore other methodological approaches to literature.

In June of 1977, I successfully defended my Ph.D. dissertation, "The Tori: Structure, Aesthetics and Time in Krio Oral-Narrative Performance." My committee comprised the following professors: Edris Makward, Harold Scheub, Neil Skinner, all from the Department of African Languages and Literature, Steven Feierman of the History Department, and Frederic G. Cassidy of the English Department. I deposited a copy of my dissertation with the Library of the University of Sierra Leone in recognition of the support that they had given me and for the promotion of future studies on Krio oral narrative traditions. I left Madison for Kano, Nigeria where I had accepted a teaching position at Bayero University-Kano. I had been in North America for a long while and welcomed the opportunity to have an experience on the African continent outside of Sierra Leone.

Student friends at Madison included but are not limited to the following: Alphonse Kwawisi Tekpetey, (Kwaku Ananse as I affectionately called him, a nickname that stuck.) He completed a Ph.D. in African Languages and Literature and taught at universities in Ghana and the Ivory Coast and now teaches at Central State University in Wilberforce, Ohio. Deirdre Lapin completed a Ph.D. in African Languages and Literature, specialising in Yoruba oral narrative traditions. She has undertaken extensive

---

[28] . "Lan buk," which is the Krio equivalent of "pursuing one's studies."

research in primary health care and development in Nigeria. She also served as the UNICEF Director in Benin. Ron Rassner, completed a Ph.D. and taught at Beloit College in Beloit, Wisconsin and at Yale University, New Haven, Connecticut. Terry Magel, completed a Ph.D. in African Languages and Literature, and teaches at the University of Western Illinois in Macomb, Illinois. Charles Pike, completed a Ph.D. in African Languages and Literature and now teaches at the University of Minnesota. Donald Cosentino completed a Ph.D. in African Languages and Literature and teaches at the University of California at Los Angeles, Syl Cheney Coker, Sierra Leonean writer, poet, novelist, and critic taught at several universities in the United States and Africa, and commutes between Sierra Leone and the United States. Joseph Lurie, completed a master's degree and now lives in Berkeley, California, where he is Executive Director Emeritus of the University of California Berkeley's International House. Okello Oculi, Ugandan writer, poet, and critic, completed a Ph.D. in Political Science and taught at Ahmadu Bello University in Kaduna, Nigeria, now lives with his family in Abuja, Nigeria. Ibrahim Mukoshy, (affectionately called Mallam), completed a Ph.D. in Linguistics and lives in Abuja and is a former colleague of mine at Bayero University, Kano, Nigeria. Cecil Blake completed a Ph.D. in Mass Communications and now teaches at the University of Pittsburgh. Oluropo Sekoni, completed a Ph.D. in African Languages and Literature, specialising on Wole Soyinka, and taught at the University of Ilorin and Lincoln University in Pennsylvania for years and has retired to his homeland in Nigeria. Mbye Cham, one of my best men at my wedding, completed a Ph.D. in African Languages and Literature and heads the African Studies Programme at Howard University, Tereffe Asrat, completed a Ph.D. in African Languages and Literature and lives in Buffalo, New York with his family. Natalie Eleady-Cole, completed a Ph.D. in Education. She taught at Fourah Bay University and now lives in the United Kingdom. Corinne and Vincent

Pelletier, Corinne, a former student of the Department of African Languages, is now a medical doctor and Vincent is a Professor of French at the University of Vermont. They both live in Vermont; Joko Sengova completed a Ph.D. in African Languages and Literature, specialising in Linguistics and taught at the University of Tampa, in Tampa, Florida; and Lemon Lappia who completed a Ph. D. in Geography and runs a consulting service in Sierra Leone.

PART THREE: FULL CIRCLE

Chapter: 14

"Sannu da Zuwa"[29]
In the Land of the Emirs

(A) Bayero University-Kano

I had been living in North America (the United States and Canada) for a long time and the pull to return to Africa had become very strong. Although I was again offered a temporary appointment in my Department at the University of Wisconsin, I decided to forgo the offer for an appointment in Nigeria. I arrived in Kano, following a short stay in Sierra Leone where I visited with my parents. The last time I had seen them was when I conducted field research for my Ph.D. a few years earlier. As a student in North America, I had interacted with many African students, especially at the University of Wisconsin-Madison. Through these interactions we (African students) developed a strong commitment to return to Africa to serve her people. It was a Pan Africanist sentiment. Although I was from Sierra Leone, I very much welcomed the opportunity to teach in an African country outside of Sierra Leone. I had met students from northern Nigeria in Madison who were now teaching at Bayero, Ahmadu Bello, Maiduguri, and other northern Universities. Thus, when the opportunity presented itself to teach in Kano, I did not hesitate to go.

Bayero University is located outside the walls of the ancient city of Kano. It had just achieved university status in 1977 - following separation from Ahmadu Bello University in Zaria to which it had been affiliated. It was among the seven new institutions that had been elevated to a university in the country in 1977. There was a dearth of

---

[29]. Hausa Greeting, meaning "welcome"

lecturers, and the university was actively recruiting qualified staff from all over the world. It was no wonder that there was a variety of teaching methods and approaches based on the geographical region where staff members had been trained. Most of the staff both foreign and local had received advanced degrees either in Nigeria, Great Britain, or North America. There were a few who had been trained in Eastern Europe.

My greatest satisfaction at Bayero derived from my students' eagerness for information. They pined for knowledge. My Head of Department assigned me the master's programme, giving me the opportunity to teach courses on African Oral Traditions, Modern African Literature and French, and Research Methodologies. This was very much a welcome challenge and an opening to introduce students to research methods in oral traditions. Also satisfying were the spirited discussions triggered by student reactions to characters in African literary works. For example, Ayi Kwei Armah's novel, *"Fragments"* elicited strong emotional reactions against the author whom, some felt, was being "unfair" with Baako, the central character, as he returned home from the United States without cargo (i.e., western conveniences), but only with his books and a guitar. "Please sir, I don't like Armah. How can Baako return home from America without modern amenities?" a female student asked. "Doesn't he realise he has a family waiting for him?" she further added. Some of the male students took issue with Armah for presenting "the man", the central character of *"The Beautiful Ones are not Yet Born"*, as spineless. They felt Armah had ridiculed "the man" through his mother-in-law who considered his penchant for integrity "worthless." One male student remarked, "Why doesn't the mother-in-law go and buy shoes for her grandchildren rather than disparage her son-in-law's manliness?" Furthermore, some students did not accept Senghor's Christian forgiveness of whites "Snow Upon Paris" for atrocities committed against Africans during the colonial period. Rather, they attributed his forgiveness to the French woman whom he had befriended. These lively observations were unlike the manner my American students had reacted to these characters when I taught at the University of Wisconsin. As to be expected, African students were closer to the realities that informed African works of art and better placed to react to these characters emotionally. Being close to one's reality was, nevertheless, evident in the reaction of an American student from New York who took issue with Senghor's portrayal of this city in the poem "New York". He considered Senghor's portrayal misleading and unsympathetic to New Yorkers.

My class on Oral Traditions examined methods for analysing this body of literature and my introduction of various methodologies for approaching the topic made students appreciate the richness of oral traditions. During vacations, I encouraged students to collect oral stories and histories from their respective home areas. These were analysed and later published under the title *"Ga Ta Nan,"* the Department's first literary journal. I also supervised the first set of three students for the master's degree in the Department of English and European Languages. One student received high marks from the external examiner for a well-researched and well-written thesis.

Despite these achievements, it was not easy navigating the administrative structure at Bayero. I felt I did not belong - more like an outsider looking in than an academic colleague. As a graduate student at the University of Wisconsin, I, and my student colleagues, had more say in the running of our department than I did as a Senior Lecturer at Bayero University. I guess there was a clash of expectations, maybe a clash of academic cultures between what I considered my role as a trained academic and what some of my high-ranking colleagues thought it should be. I remember raising a question for more explanation to a point that was being put forward by one of my high-ranking colleagues and getting a very unprofessional response. One of his statements to me was the following, "Dr. Broderick you are African, and I am an African." Frankly, I did not understand what he meant by the remark. Furthermore, what was more disturbing was the tone of the remark. It was as if I were a child being lectured by an adult. That evening as I walked home to my residence, a Canadian colleague who had been at the university longer than me and attended this Faculty Board Meeting gave me a lift. He said that it was not the tradition at the university to question statements by high-ranking officials. It was all right for another high-ranking official to do so. A student, let alone a senior faculty member, could have asked the observation I made. I attribute this behaviour as being the result of my religious and/or ethnic status. I was not a Muslim nor a Hausa/Fulani or northern Nigerian or Nigerian. And even though I had a Nigerian name of Yoruba origin (Modupe), it was not Hausa/Fulani. The only common trait that I had with my Nigerian colleague was my African identity and that is why he probably referred to it. The fact that we were both academics did not matter. It was not important for his concern. But being African was common ground and more important. That probably meant that I should support his point or keep my mouth shut. Had my observation been made by a European colleague, I dare say his reaction would have been different - probably more academic than ethnic or religious. Furthermore, in as much as I wanted to conduct research on northern Nigerian oral traditions, I discovered that I could not do so because of religious concerns and my gender, which limited my access to homes. I was more interested in investigating the traditions of non-Islamized societies but was later informed that I should focus my research on Islamized Societies. Despite these drawbacks, I was, nevertheless, grateful to the university for sponsoring me on two trips to the United States where I presented papers on oral traditions based on research in Sierra Leone; one was at the African Studies Association meeting in Los Angeles in 1979 and the other was at the African Literature Conference at Claremont Colleges, in Claremont, California in 1981. The university was supportive of staff members presenting papers at international academic gatherings.

As time went by, it became apparent that appreciation of one's contributions at Faculty of Arts Board meetings was based not necessarily on academic substance but rather on ones' socio-religious affiliation and ethnicity. My Nigerian colleagues who had studied in the United States did not speak out against what I may describe as "non-progressive behaviours," except one who arrogantly abused the Kano traditional elites, an act that later cost him his life. I was not opposed to "Northernisation" but rather, welcomed it. But I also felt, as a concerned academic, one should be able to present one's opinions on academic issues openly and responsibly and not in a climate of intimidation. My malaise was also experienced by other non-Nigerians lecturers (African and non-African) and many of them chose to leave the university at the expiration of their contracts. The spirit of Pan Africanism that we had cultivated in the United States was no longer a core value. There were other socio-ethnic/religious factors at play, and they were more important for the hegemony of the society. Because of these circumstances, I decided, sadly, it was time to leave, after four years at Bayero.

Socially, there were gatherings organised by Nigerian staff members, mainly southerners - only a handful of northerners socialise with us (i.e., non-Nigerian Africans) outside of official university engagement. Children's birthday parties were great occasions for adults to congregate at the home of the parents of the birthday child at the end of the birthday party. There would be delicious dishes awaiting the guests such as pounded yam and egusi soup, pepper soups, jollof rice, tsire/suya and kose, roasted lamb or goat. This would be followed by spirited discussions usually pertaining to politics in Nigeria, at the university or in one's department. Other great meeting places for socialising were the Kano and French Clubs. For example, the acquisition of a brand-new car would be a pretext for getting together. We would meet at one of these clubs, at the owner's expense to celebrate the new acquisition. The event was referred to as "Washing the Car." The Kano Club had been established during the colonial period under a national framework that included clubs in other major Nigerian cities. Its membership had been civil service employees - mainly expatriates. Thus, membership in a particular club gave a patron access to a club in another city. The Kano club had an array of members comprising middle- and upper-income professionals and more African in its composition. It also offered an array of sports facilities (tennis, golf, table tennis, cricket, football,) and an outdoor movie theatre that showed mainly American movies. I made it a point to go to the Kano Club on a Tuesday afternoon for lunch, as I knew the menu had egusi and pounded yam with stockfish, a dish that I enjoyed very much. Accordingly, I would make the ten-mile round-trip from the University to the Kano Club for this specialty. The French Club, on the other hand, was more selective in its membership and comprised mainly of upper income professionals and expatriates. The menu was more upscale, and the music more sophisticatedly presented. The venue was always very populated on Saturday evenings and there would always be a dance following dinner. There was also a Lebanese Club. However, its membership was more restricted to the Lebanese Community and during my four years in Kano I only went there three times as the guest of a patron. If these social outlets were not sufficient, one could always frequent the low-income entertainment spots in Sabon Gari (New Towns), mainly inhabited by southern Nigerians.

During the long break, June, July August, I usually travelled to Sierra Leone to visit my parents, relatives, and friends for three weeks and then continue to the United States. One of the striking features that would catch my eye on arriving in Freetown was the very lush vegetation compared to the dryness of Northern Nigeria. The green forest that populated the hills of Freetown and the Sierra Leone peninsular presented an awesome view. Later, when I worked in Guinea and often travelled to Freetown by road from Conakry, the scenic beauty of the misty hills of the peninsular, which majestically appeared in the distance as one approached the town of Songo, would strike me. I often wondered what the view was like at the time when the early

European explorers and slave traders sailed up the Sierra Leone River to Bunce Island for enslaved Africans or at the time when the settlers from Nova Scotia and Jamaica arrived? It must have been an even more spectacular view then. Regretfully, a lot of these forests are being cut down today due to uncontrolled urbanisation.

(B) Mai Tatsine Riots

Kano played a critical role in the Trans-Saharan trade. Often one would see scores of camels, which had crossed the Sahara or were getting ready to go across, parked in various areas of the city. Not far from Bayero University was the wall city of old Kano with its maze of markets, an area frequented by tourists looking for exotic leather works and jewellery. I also enjoyed visiting neighbouring towns/villages on their market days. On such occasions, I would buy lovely bedspreads, at bargain prices, that had been woven by skilled craftsmen. I also enjoyed eating hot grilled "Tsire/Suya" - (Spiced Kebabs) as well as freshly prepared "Kose" (fried bean cake-akara) spiced with hot pepper which were available at the markets.

In December of 1980, the peace of Kano was disrupted by the Mai Tatsine Riots that engulfed the city. Followers of this breakaway Muslim sect were killing orthodox Muslims for wearing watches and other "western decorations" which they considered "forbidden/un-Islamic." The day the riots broke out I had driven a friend to the airport in the morning and decided to take a different route back to the campus from the route that I had taken earlier. Later, I discovered that my decision had been wise. Had I taken the route that had brought me to the airport, I would have been caught in the riots. On the advice of the university authorities the staff stayed on campus and dared not venture into the city. When the Kano police aided by the Nigerian military had brought the rioting under control, we were given the green light to venture into the city. A group of us decided to drive in a convoy into the city for provisions not realising that there were vigilante groups in various areas. We had hardly gone two miles when we ran into the first vigilante group whose members were stopping cars and demanding that the passengers descend for inspection. The vigilantes were looking for followers of the religious sect whom they alleged had indelible blue marks on their navels, and ankles. The vigilantes were armed with spears and machetes and one false move or open resistance could result in death. I politely told the vigilantes that we were lecturers at Bayero University and so were the passengers in the two other vehicles behind me. I then complied with their demands by raising my shirt to expose my navel and raising my pants to show my ankles. They wanted to do the same to a female passenger but when I protested, they left her alone. I was the driver of the lead car of our convoy and due to my cooperation; the passengers in other vehicles were not inspected. As we drove down the road from the university, which parallels the walls of the old city, we saw numerous burnt bodies on the roadside. At another site, we saw the body of a young boy who had been freshly hacked to death. This sight was ghastly, and we decided to return to the campus as we had seen enough.

Prior to leaving Nigeria in August of 1981, there were a spate of riots in Kano and one of them took the life of a former lecturer at Bayero University who espoused Marxism. He became very political and engaged in public condemnations on radio and television of traditional elites. Rioters entered his house, killed him, and burnt his body. Being an elite from the ruling house of Bauchi did not help in sparing his life. Today, northern Nigeria is plagued by the Boko Haram movement whose members have killed non-Muslims and Muslims across north-eastern Nigeria in such towns as Maiduguri, Kano, Jos and Abuja. Supporters of Boko Haram are followers of the Mai Tatsine rioters of the early eighties'.

Educationally and socially, I do not regret having gone to northern Nigeria. Had I not gone; I would not have been able to appreciate what I experienced. It was a rich learning experience, and I made a lot of friends.

Chapter: 15

Baiacu, Itaparica Island, Bahia Brazil
– An Interlude

In August of 1981, I married Amelia Ayodele Fitzjohn whom I had known since my youth. Her parents and my parents were friends, and her father had served as the first Sierra Leonean Charge d'Affaires at the Embassy of Sierra Leone in Washington DC. She was on assignment to Brasilia, Brazil as a Foreign Service Officer with the United States Information Service, as it was known then, based with the United States Embassy in Brasilia. While in Brasilia I tried to gain employment with one of the universities in Brasilia but was unsuccessful. I was offered a position at the American School to teach Social Science subjects, mainly History and Geography. Geography had been one of my favourite subjects in Secondary School and so was History, and I had majored in History and Government for my BA degree at Otterbein University. During my second term at the school, I headed the Social Science and Humanities Departments and one of my colleagues was a Canadian Art Teacher. During discussions, she found out about my work on African Oral Traditions at the University of Wisconsin-Madison, and she told me that she would like for me to meet her husband who was a diplomat in the Canadian Embassy. One of his responsibilities was the provision of funds in various areas of development to Brazilian Non-Governmental Organisations. Through him I got funded to teach and conduct research in San Salvador da Bahia, a city with a very high percentage of Afro-Brazilians. I very much welcomed the change and resigned my position at the American School.

While also in Brasilia, I took a course on Photography from Kenton Keith who was the Deputy Director of the United States Information Agency in Brazil, and a colleague of my wife. Kenton, a master photographer, had created a darkroom in the basement of his house for developing films and making prints. He immersed himself in photography as a serious pastime. As for me, I had always been interested in photography and had started shooting pictures, mainly portraits, since my secondary school days in Sierra Leone, with a box camera that my mother had acquired during her student days in England. However, I had no knowledge of the principles of the art form or the technical operation of a camera to produce effects. The requirements for the course were that each student own a manual camera, (preferably a 35mm SLR) attend classes regularly, and pay the costs for developing and printing of films.

About a dozen of us Foreign Service Officers and spouses took the training over a period of three months and met once every week at Kenton's house. Kenton started the course by doing a historical presentation of photography, highlighting the great masters of the genre and their techniques. The focus of the course was on black and white photography, with an emphasis on the aesthetics of composition and interpretation of scenes, the manipulation of light, adjusting film speed and how that affects or enhances the quality of the picture, and the creation of depth of field through the control of aperture (F-Stops) and shutter speed. Approaching photography as an art form, based on the principles of communication, was very similar to understanding how a literary work (novel, poem. play or oral narrative) is put together to produce meaning. This aspect has been a major focus of my academic training in the study of oral narratives. Following the discussions of the principles of photography, Kenton then tasked us with practical assignments. We were required to take pictures of scenes and objects in and around Brasilia to demonstrate our knowledge of these principles or how to produce aesthetic effects to enhance a scene. He had arranged for a photography store to develop the films and make prints, which he would critique to provide us feedback. To enhance my photographic skills, I subscribed to journals such as *Aperture, Shutterbug, Photography Today,* etc., where I read articles on various aspects of the art form. I was glad that I had the opportunity to take the course as the skills acquired have stood me in good stead. For example, while in Benin, I taught a course on photography to my co-workers at USAID on how this medium can be used as a tool for monitoring projects. Daily, I took both black and white and colour pictures of my daughter, who was then two months old. I did this to document her growth, as well as to record for posterity picturesque scenes and objects of my stay in Brazil. In Benin I befriended a Beninese photographer and together, we used to go out shooting market scenes and events in Cotonou and Porto Novo, etc. Kenton's son, Vincent, who lives in London, UK, is a successful professional photographer. No doubt, he acquired the basic skills of his métier from his father.

From September of 1983 to June of 1984, I was engaged by the University of Bahia to teach Anthropological Research Methods to third-year students at the University. I had lived in Brazil for almost two years and had acquired Portuguese from language courses taught at the United States Embassy and through my interactions with Brazilians. I also had a proficient knowledge of French which facilitated understanding the grammatical structure and vocabulary of Portuguese, another Latin-derived (Romance) language. The task of teaching was challenging as I considered my Portuguese language skills rudimentary for teaching at the university level. Nevertheless, my students were gracious enough to spare me a sense of guilt for murdering their language. As I had conducted research on oral-narratives traditions in Sierra Leone, I was interested in doing a similar study in Bahia, Brazil, primarily to examine the strong African cultural input.

In the city of San Salvador da Bahia dos Todos Os Santos (commonly referred to as Salvador da Bahia), the presence of Africa is overwhelming. I had never seen the like in the United States or Canada, countries with significant African populations and where I had lived on the North American continent. The African cultural presence manifested itself in the cuisine, folklore, song and dance (Capoeira[30]) and would be displayed on festive occasions such as candomble[31] and carnival ceremonies. For example, in Bahia there was a school that specialises in teaching the martial art of capoeira to young Brazilians. Enslaved Africans had used Capoeira as a means of self-defence against slaveholders during the nineteenth century. The strongest African presence in Bahia was from the Yoruba ethnic group of Nigeria, Benin and Togo. This was exhibited in such foods as acaraje (bean cake - literally "eat akara" in Yoruba) dende (palm oil), mokoto (a dish made of farinia/gari, (grated cassava), and parts of the foot of a cow), and mukeka, (a spicy dish made of fish cooked in palm oil with onions and green peppers and cocoa-nut milk). I became friends with a Brazilian student (Antonio) whom I had met through an African American friend. I told him of my research interests, and he recommended I visit a fishing village on the Island of Itaparica whose inhabitants would probably be able to help. My new friend also knew the island and was building a small house on it.

One Sunday morning, Antonio and I boarded the ferry from Salvador, with my car, to explore Itaparica Island. The side of the island that faced the city of Bahia was developed, graced with lovely beaches, villas, and beach houses. The opposite side of the island was very poor, rural in many ways, and it was on this side that Baiacu was located. We drove on a dirt road to the village, through forest vegetation. As we proceeded, I got the feeling of being in West Africa, and when we arrived and I saw the villagers, my thoughts of being back in a West African seaside village were confirmed. Further contacts with the villagers revealed they

---

[30] . A martial art from Angola
[31] . Afro-Brazilian religion of African origin

were economically more disadvantaged than their counterparts in West Africa. We made several Sunday visits to the village to establish a rapport with the villagers. I would go to the village dressed in blue jeans, carrying a bag in which I had a tape recorder, several cameras, batteries and films, and my pipe, etc. With their permission, I would take pictures of villagers and fishermen pulling in their haul. Children would also follow me around requesting their pictures to be taken. We made several such exploratory visits during which I would ask questions concerning the existence of an oral-narrative tradition. Then, a middle-aged man consented to talk with us about stories, and we fixed a date for the following Sunday to meet him and friends at his house. On the day of the appointment, Antonio and I arrived at his house at the agreed time. We thanked our host for receiving us, and I took out my equipment to start recording. No sooner had I done so than two stocky-build men, in plain clothes, entered the house and interrupted the discussion - ordering Antonio and me to follow them to the police station. Antonio protested and asked what had we done wrong? They responded that we were thieves as there had been a theft everywhere my car had been seen on the island. A heated exchange then ensued between Antonio and the police officers. Antonio looked at me and said, "do you know why they are doing this to us?" I responded "No" He quickly added, "it is because we are blacks." I said, "but they are blacks too," although there was a range in the colour pigmentation of the villagers starting from high yellow to jet-black.[32] He said that it did not matter. I told Antonio to tell them that we would go to the police station, which was about a three-mile drive from the village. I told them we would drive behind them to the

---

[32] . I note this observation because colour pigmentation and wealth in Brazil determine upward social mobility. Furthermore, unlike the U.S. were having 1% of black blood makes a person "black", the situation is the opposite in Brazil; 1% of white blood makes the person "white."

station. The men said they did not have transportation and requested a ride with us.[33] We bade farewell to my host and thanked him and his friends for their hospitality. We could tell that my host was visibly shaken by the incident. We arrived at the station and met the Police Chief. The room reeked of cachaca, (the local Brazilian rum) and stale smoke from an ashtray cluttered with cigarette butts. Antonio told him who we were and the purpose of our visit to the island. While he and Antonio conversed, I lit my pipe and started puffing. He looked at me from the corner of his eye and then continued talking with Antonio. I guess he wondered about this black man who dared to smoke a pipe in his presence! The Police Chief said that the villagers had reported thefts everywhere my car had been seen on the island, and that they did not understand what the CD Plates meant. I then told him that I was from the American Embassy in Brasilia, and I was a Professor at the University of Bahia—an unlikely story for him as it was not common for Blacks to occupy such positions.[34] The Police Chief then requested my identity papers. I took out my diplomatic card, issued by the Brazilian Ministry of Foreign Affairs (Itamaraty), and gave it to him. He looked at the card, and after a long pause, he responded, "I respect this, I respect this. I respect this." Then he said, "but why didn't you not come here before to introduce yourself so I would alert the villagers." This was a question that I had posed to Antonio, once before, and he told me that it was not necessary for us to do so, that he knew the island and its inhabitants. I had told him that the procedure outlined by the Police Chief was

---

[33]. I guess this was a way to make sure we did not get away, although, in truth, they had no other means of getting to the Police Station on a Sunday other than by walking. I suspect they also wanted to make sure that the Police Chief saw my car's CD licence plate.

[34]. Indeed, I recall when I was teaching my classes at the university and someone would walk by and noticed me. The person would stop and turn around to make sure his eyes had seen right. This happened several times.

exactly the method I had adopted during my field research in Sierra Leone, that I would commence my dialogues with villagers by first meeting with the Village Chief or Headman or Headwoman to introduce myself. Now that my identity had been confirmed and we were no longer thieves, the Police Chief then asked us to join him in his cachaca. We politely refused and thanked him for his offer. But somehow, as to be expected, we got into a discussion on Brazil's favourite pastime subject - football (soccer). I told him I was a supporter of Flamengo, (a Rio de Janeiro-based team) which turned out to be his favourite team also. Through football and being a supporter of his team, I had become his friend. He bade us good-bye and assured me that I could continue with my research and that if I encountered any other problem, I should come and see him.

Brazilian fanaticism for football and their no-love-loss attitude against their arch football rival (Argentina) was best captured in the remark of a taxi driver, in Brasilia, who gave me a ride home during the 1982 Football World Cup in Spain. As I was exiting his car he said to me, "you are my last customer for the day. I'm going home now to get ready for the football match between Argentina and Brazil. We're going to teach these Argentinians that they do not know how to fight a war (reference to the war between Argentina and Great Britain over the Falkland Islands}, nor do they know how to play football." Indeed, the taxi driver's prophecy came to pass. Brazil won the match and Argentina lost the war to Great Britain. The rivalry between these two South American football giants is very much alive and intense, and cuts across economics and development. It is also racial due to the high population of blacks in Brazil compared to Argentina, whose blacks have been exterminated, making Argentinians feel more European because they are less mixed with black blood and thus "culturally superior." It is estimated that sixty percent of Brazilians have black blood in their veins.

Antonio and I drove back to the village and dropped off the two police assistants who had accompanied us. They never uttered a word to us on the ride back, no apology acknowledging their mistake. I then went by the house of the villager with whom we had the appointment. He apologised again for what had transpired and invited Antonio and me to lunch at his house the following Sunday. We thanked him for his invitation and told him we would be there.

That evening upon my return to my apartment in Salvador, I called my wife in Brasilia and told her I had just been let out of jail (of course I was exaggerating). She was no doubt concerned about the mishap but later when she heard the whole story, we laughed about it. The following Sunday, Antonio and I returned to our host. He had prepared a lovely meal for us. We ate heartily and were touched by his humanity. He said that he was very much embarrassed by what had happened the previous Sunday and that he was not aware of the plan initiated by the two men to arrest us. We told him not to worry about it, and that we were very grateful for his hospitality. I reported the incident to my wife's colleague, (the Branch Public Affairs Officer) at the Consulate in Bahia who reported it to the Consular General. My wife's colleague observed, "I go out all the time to Itaparica with a CD licence plate and have never been arrested," then he quickly added "I'm white and that makes a big difference in Brazil."

I subsequently collected a few narratives. Although the narratives were presented orally, I discovered on further investigation that they had been acquired from a written text. The stories that the villagers told had been produced in a text that someone else had read to them and which they retold. This procedure was very much unlike the oral-narrative tradition that I had worked with in Africa, where stories were learned from oral performers. There had been no written text. Storytellers acquired their story-telling skills at an early age by observing skilled artists perform, and through practice became successful performers. In this manner the tradition is passed orally from one generation to the next. During our discussions, I told the villagers I was from Sierra Leone, a country in Africa. One old man asked, "where is Africa?" I told him that it was on the other side of the sea. He said that he knew his origins were from Africa, but he did not know where Africa was. I was moved by his question and remark. Antonio and I returned to Baiacu for several more visits, and the villagers received us cordially.

I cannot close this incident without narrating another incident which took place at the American Consulate in Bahia and which almost cost me my life. I had gone to the Consulate to finish a report that I was going to submit to the University of Bahia. I was still working at closing time and the secretary told me to close the door when I left. Unfortunately, no one told the guard, stationed at the hallway of the building, that I was upstairs working. After I completed the report, I closed the door and proceeded to the stairs. As I descended the two flights to the street level hallway entrance, I lit my pipe and continued to puff at it. When the guard heard the footsteps descending, he immediately thought it was a thief and he drew out his pistol. Then he saw a black man smoking a pipe merrily descending the stairs. Seeing the pistol, I quickly said to him in my halting Portuguese that I was from the American Embassy in Brasilia, and that I was working on a report. I do not know whether he believed me or not. But when he heard my accent and saw me with a pipe, and I was not carrying any merchandise that would be stolen, he became less perturbed. He said, "No one told me that you were up there." We exchanged pleasantries and I wished him good night, thanking my stars that he had remained calm and there had been no altercation.

The next day when I returned to the consulate, I was greeted with remarks pertaining to the incident of the previous evening. The secretaries were joking about this black thief who was smoking a pipe as he departed the consulate. I said, "This is nothing to laugh about. I could have been killed. You guys should have told the guard that

I was up there working when you departed the building yesterday."

"Yes", they said, "you are right, but we forgot."

There were other American scholars undertaking research or teaching at the University. One of them, Ibrahim Sundiata, became a good friend of mine. He is currently a Professor of African and Brazilian Studies at Brandeis University. He, being an Historian and I, being an Anthropologist, had very fruitful discussions on Afro-Brazilian culture and traditions. I also had the opportunity of meeting Professor Anani Dzidzienyo of Brown University whose brother Vishnu Wassiamal had been the Ghanaian Ambassador to Brazil. Anani and I would also become good friends, and he invited me to Brown to give a lecture to his students on my research in Bahia. I also became a friend of Professor Libene Boulivi of the Universite du Benin in Lome, Togo. He was teaching Ewe and conducting research on African lexical items in Afro-Brazilian communities in the northeast of Brazil.

In Brasilia I also became friends with Kofi Awoonor who replaced Vishnu Wassiamal as the Ghanaian Ambassador to Brazil. Ambassador Wassiamal had introduced me to Professor Michael Turner of Hunter College in New York. At that time, Professor Turner was affiliated with the Ford Foundation based in Rio de Janeiro. It was always a pleasure visiting Professor Turner in Rio. He was well integrated into Brazilian society at all levels. Later, we met in Benin where my wife was assigned. Professor Turner had done his Ph.D. dissertation for Boston University on the Brazilians who had returned to Benin during the 19th century. He and Professors Sundiata and Dzidzienyo were very good friends, and I considered myself very fortunate to have joined their circle of friends. Another American who was conducting research on Brazilian Popular Art was Barbara Browning of Yale University. She was supported by a Fulbright Fellowship to study Afro-Brazilian dance. She is now an accomplished novelist, dancer and cultural critic who lives in New York City where she teaches at the Tisch School of the Arts at New York University. My Bahian experience had thus afforded me a wealth of scholarly interpersonal exchanges with Bahian and American scholars.

Every year, during the period November to March, there are several festivals in various communities of the city of Bahia. These festivals could be considered "warm-up sessions" in preparation for the famous Salvador carnival in late February or early March. I attended all of them and took a lot of pictures, some of which I have mounted. I spent a profitable year at the University of Bahia and very much enjoyed my work. Often my wife and our 12-month-old daughter, at the time, would come for weekend visits. I would take them sightseeing and explore Bahian communities. She and I partook heartily of the Afro-Brazilian cuisine and other cultural events, including dancing with our daughter in the famous Salvador carnival. Brazilians are a vivacious people with a vibrant sense of humour and a joie de vivre that is infectious. They enjoy life to its fullest - other than football nothing bothers them. They are proud of who they are. A Brazilian friend remarked that when General De Gaulle, President of France, visited Brazil, he said at the conclusion of his visit that Brazilians were not serious people. My friend retorted, "De Gaulle was right, because if we are serious, we won't be Brazilians." Our daughter, Vania, was born in Brazil. She is our Brazilian gift--a treasured remembrance of our delightful three-year stay in that country.

Chapter: 16

"Meme les Blancs Passent par Ici", Et "C'est Nous d'Abord qui Avons Vu les Blancs"

Upon our return from Brazil to the United States, my spouse had to acquire French in preparation for her assignment as the American Embassy Public Affairs Officer to the Republic of Benin. While in Washington, I was employed by the Foreign Service Institute and by the African Development Foundation on a part time basis. At the Foreign Service Institute, I was chairperson of Francophone African Studies charged with the responsibility of teaching African Literature and culture to Foreign Service Officers who were going to serve in French-speaking countries in Africa. At the African Development Foundation my French language skills enabled me to offer counsel on projects that had been submitted in French for funding from francophone African countries. While my spouse was on assignment to the Republic of Benin, and Cote d'Ivoire I was employed by USAID on a contract to manage projects, which gave me the opportunity to travel widely in these countries. I was able to observe the attitudes and behaviours of Africans as they interacted with one another and with me.

Two anecdotes are presented below as they shed light on the impact of colonialism on the discourse of Africans.

They are entitled (A) "Même les blancs passent par ici" "Even whites enter through this gate" and (B) "C'est nous d'abord qui avons vu les blancs." "We were the first to interact with Europeans." These two anecdotes were uttered by ordinary Africans; story (A) by a Beninese guard who monitored the entrance to a house inhabited by a colleague of mine and story (B) by an Ivorian driver of an international donor for which I worked. The context and analysis of these utterances follow.

Story A

A colleague of mine was travelling to the United States, and I seized the opportunity to have him take a few letters for mailing. Upon arrival at his house, my very first visit, I proceeded to enter the house through the main gate. I knocked at the gate and waited for it to be opened by the guard. A voice came from the other side requesting that I go to a side gate. I then realised that there was a side entrance, not easily visible, smaller than the main entrance from which the house could be entered. I introduced myself and informed the guard that I had come to see his master who later gave him the green light to let me in. As I went through, I apologised for the mishap and explained to him that this was my first time to the house and was not aware that there was a secondary gate, which was the preferred entrance. He quickly retorted, "Monsieur, même les blancs passent par ici." "Sir, even the white guests enter through this entrance." I was bemused by his remark and told him I will remember his advice on my next visit.

Comments: What is significant about this story is the guard's injection of race into the dialogue, which was unwarranted. As he could have simply told me the side gate was the preferred entrance, his racial reference is at best troubling—and at worst self-destructive. Even though I told him that this was my very first visit, which he ignored, he was baffled as to why I should want to go through the main entrance when white guests used the side entrance. Had I been white, he probably would have said, "Monsieur, ca c'est la porte que l'on utilise." (Sir, this is the entrance that we use.") Who knows, he may have let me in without saying a word. The question then arises as to why he injected race in his response, as we were both blacks? Was he trying to tell me something? Why should I make the "forbidden mistake" of entering through the main gate when whites entered through the secondary gate? Had I been upper class Beninese, he probably would have acted differently, obsequiously informing me that the side gate is the entrance preferred. Maybe, he thought, the explanation given should enthral me, as this was the gate used by whites. In other words, I should be pleased about entering the compound through the same gates used by whites. Maybe, had he known that I was a foreigner and a colleague of his master; he may have excused my ignorance. But in the context in which the discourse started, how does one explain his remark? I attribute his response to the destruction of self that colonised people undergo. In his mind, the main gate should be the entrance used by whites, but since they were not using this gate, no black person should be allowed to use the main gate. It should be noted that his master was white which may have given him an added air of self-importance in his relationship with black Beninese of his class. Maybe he was not accustomed to blacks visiting his master's house. Likely, his worldview of whites and Africans had been shaped by the dichotomized socio-economic relationship between these two groups in terms of economic power and race.

Story B

I had travelled to Yamoussoukro to participate in a workshop held at one of the colleges of this political capital of the Ivory Coast. While there, my American and Ivorian colleagues and I, marvelled at the quality of the workmanship of the buildings and the modern facilities and equipment of the college where the workshop was held. The rooms were well furnished with beautiful desks and wardrobes, lovely beds, and beautiful bathrooms. The same could be said of the cafeteria, which was fully furnished and well maintained. I dare say that the furnishings were more upscale than what would be found in many American college dormitories. Following the conclusion of the workshop, my colleagues and I visited the newly completed Basilica built by President Houphouet Boigny. The building was stupendous and truly a wonder to behold. We also noted how well planned the city of Yamoussoukro was, graced with boulevards large enough to land a Boeing 747. On the drive back to Abidjan my colleagues and I were commenting on the magnificent Basilica, and President Boigny's achievements. It was then the driver quipped:

> "Mais tout ça, c'est pour rien. Les gens de Yamoussoukro n'apprécient pas ça. Ils vivent dans la brousse. Tous ces édifices devaient être construits à Abidjan ou dans les villes qui longent la côte. Après tout, c'est nous d'abord qui avons vu les blancs."

> Translation: "Eh, all of this is worthless. The people of Yamoussoukro cannot appreciate all these buildings and modernization. They are forest people. These buildings should have been built in Abidjan or in towns along the coast. After all, it is we (the people of the coastal region of the Ivory Coast) who first interacted with the white man."

I knew the driver well. I had travelled with him before on several occasions on long trips during which he conversed openly about Ivorian politics and other contemporary matters. He enjoyed expressing his views. He was from a coastal town not far from Abidjan. He was a southerner as opposed to Ivoirians who hailed from the middle belt such as the President, who was from Yamoussoukro or Ivoirians from the North.

Comments:

Two points should be made here: (1) the colonial impact and (2) the ethno-political context. About the first, the driver is a southerner from one of the coastal towns of the Ivory Coast. Europeans came across the seas and brought western civilization through religion and education to the coastal peoples of Africa. Thus, colonial towns were built and became the administrative centres of the imperial powers. In the case of the Ivory Coast three coastal towns have served as the political capital of the country: Grand Bassam, Bingerville, and Abidjan. It was from these coastal cities that the social and political elites of these countries were first established. It was much later in the colonial experience that western education and traditions penetrated the interior from the colonial centres.

The ethno-political context, the second point, serves to demonstrate the impact of colonialism on the mindset of the driver and fellow Ivoirians. Given that southern Ivoirians "benefitted" first from the colonial experience, they are, in the mind of the driver, "entitled beneficiaries." For him it is a right that should be accorded to his people because of their early exposure to westernisation. Accordingly, they should be the beneficiaries because of their "privilege status" as opposed to their "unfortunate" brethren who happened to be born in the interior. Because of his southern roots, the driver considers himself ethnically superior to President Boigny and his people. As outsiders to the Ivory Coast, he probably felt that we (my American colleagues and I) supported his opinion. He could not see or chose not to appreciate the President's achievement as a national success and the jobs that the upgrading of Yamoussoukro and the building of the Basilica created for Ivoirians and other nationals of the sub-region. For him and Ivoirians who think like him, such achievements, tantamount to casting pearls to swine, should be in the south and not in Yamoussoukro, a city of the middle belt.

I saw a similar attitude, manifested in the opposite direction, in northern Nigeria where Islam had come across the Sahara as early as the eighth century, establishing centres of scholarship in various towns across the Sahel. Because of this early contact with Islam which predated the westernization of coastal towns on the African continent, (except for the Islamic contact on the East African coast), people from the Sahel regions consider themselves superior to and look down on their brethren from coastal and forest areas. Indeed, Arabs living in North Africa do not consider themselves as being Africans or their countries being in

Africa. Africa for them is south of the Sahara. I recall a Moroccan on a BBC radio programme trying to tell the audience where his country was located. Not once did he ever mention that his country was in Africa or Northwest Africa to be more precise. Rather, he said that his country was located south of Spain. In another BBC programme, a Zimbabwean on a motorbike adventure from London to Cape Town said he was astonished to discover from locals in Tangier, Morocco, when he crossed from Gibraltar that he was not yet in Africa. It was not until he crossed the Sahara would he be in Africa. I also witnessed a manifestation of the attitude of the Ivorian driver in Sierra Leone as a teenager when a large church was built in Taiama and a large hotel (Adams) was built in Magburaka, both towns outside of the western area which used to be known as the colony as opposed to the protectorate (the interior). For the inhabitants of the western area of Sierra Leone, where the colonial capital is located, they could not fathom the idea of such "grandiose" buildings being erected outside of Freetown. They derisively referred to the church as a "Cathedral in the Bush" and to the hotel as "Bush Hotel." In Benin, where I also worked, some inhabitants of the southern citadels of Porto Novo and Ouidah could not fathom the idea of a city from Brazil being twinned with the town of Parakou in the north.

There is a third dimension to these anecdotes. It has to do with constructive leadership. Development calls for constructive sensitization enacted through a national policy that has been successfully vetted through civil society groups. Oftentimes, development is perceived by nationals through a regional or ethnic lens and not through a national vision. An important task at hand is for leaders to start laying the foundation for constructive development to take place to produce the desired national economic growth. Obviously, for this equation to be solved there must be regional balance. For example, if oil is being produced in a certain region, it would make sense for the benefits of this commodity to be shared in the region from which it is extracted as well as with other areas of the country. In my opinion President Boigny addressed this issue in a practical manner when he developed educational centres of excellence on a regional basis. Liberal Arts and medical schools were established in Abidjan, a city of the south. Yamoussoukro, a town of the middle belt, hosted the engineering centres and Aboisso, a town of the eastern fertile region, was made the agricultural centre. President Kwame Nkrumah had achieved a similar feat by establishing the University of Science and Technology in Kumasi, a town of the middle belt in Ghana and the University of Legon in Accra.

Chapter: 17

The African Intelligentsia and Behaviours

The thoughts expressed in this chapter derive from my international development experience over the last 26 years in Africa. Its purpose is to invite development experts and other critical thinkers (the African intelligentsia e.g., Politicians, Academics, Religious Leaders, Civil Servants, University Students) to participate in open debates (national discussion/dialogue) or conduct research on societal behaviours that affect national development. It is important for such an undertaking to take place, particularly in countries that have experienced national conflicts and are undergoing reconstruction. The challenge, however, is not limited only to post-conflict countries but also apply to those African countries in which successful national development programmes have been implemented. Countries that have been able to achieve a better quality of life as demonstrated by positive social indicators in such areas as Rule of Law, Governance, Peace and Security, Health, Education, Economic Growth, Social Welfare of Children, and Youth Empowerment are appropriate models of positive societal behaviour and can serve as case studies for investigation and emulation. Scholars who wish to pursue research in this area might find Myonnie Bada's model a useful analytical framework for such an undertaking.[35] In this paper Bada makes two critical distinctions between culture and social structures. "Culture, in and of itself, is a uniquely human trait. As a vehicle of human expression, it cannot exist apart from

---

[35]. Myonnie Bada, "Culture and Social Structures," For presentation at the 44th Annual International Studies Association Convention, February 25-March 1, 2003, accessed November 07, 2012,
https://isanet.ccit.arizona.edu/portlandarchives/bada.html

human society, and likewise, no human society can exist without it. It is an expression of identity recognizable in every form of communication, be it through language, music, literature, art, dance, and even cuisine. And as much as it is an expression of identity, it is something by which we can identify certain cultures, although currently of advanced globalisation (bear in mind that cultural exchange has been taking place ever since humans began wandering the planet), many cultural traits have been exchanged and adopted among peoples to the extent that they can no longer be indicative of a single culture." In short Culture is "the sum of a people's common experiences, values, preferences, and behavioural tendencies, which have been shaped by a common history and which guides interaction and expression among these people". [36]

"Social structures are those arrangements of human relations which place everyone into an appropriate place in society, which either defines or is defined by her/his function. *Social structures*, in conjunction with cultural beliefs, determine the types of accepted relationships among members of a cultural society." "Social structures are greatly influenced by culture in addition to other influences, such as economic and political conditions."[37]

The above citations are introduced as a means for scholars/academics to pursue long-term/on-going research in this area. However, for the short-term, i.e., the foreseeable future, I would like for civil society leaders (religious and non-religious, politicians, academics, college students, and critical thinkers - the intelligentsia) to actively engage freely in this dialogue and not to be bound by Myonnie Bada's analytical model. Participants in this debate are free to choose other analytical models deemed useful for their investigations. A product of the interaction of these two categories postulated by Bada is behaviour, the subject matter of this discussion presented below. I am

---

[36] . Ibid
[37] . Ibid

sceptical as to whether my proposed undertaking will attract the "immediate" attention of politicians and or civil servants as its focus calls for self-analysis, and we humans do not like to self-scrutinise for fear of the results that might be revealed. Accordingly, we remain in denial, hoping that the issues we recognize as problems will go away or that someone will come to help us make them go away. But unfortunately, the problems do not go away, rather they continue to fester and multiply. In addition, given the bitter civil strife that some African countries have undergone since independence, I would argue that it is paramount that national leaders and critical thinkers, alike, analyse their societies in the interest of finding common-sense solutions to issues affecting civil rights/others' rights and behaviour to put measures in place to improve the quality of life of their citizens. I would submit that this type of analysis should be an on-going integrated process for all sectors, necessary for the welfare of the nation. And it is not as if this tradition was non-existent in Africa. For example, we had personalities such as Bai Bureh, Lamina Sankoh, ITA Wallace Johnson, Kwame Nkrumah, Frantz Fanon, Edward Wilmot Blyden, and Amical Cabral, to name but a few, who were vigorous analysts and whose contributions played a key role in the struggle for independence. They were nationalists fighting for the betterment of their people. By the same token, we need members of the intelligentsia to embrace the spirit of the above personalities and analyse the post-colonial era to pinpoint problems that led to the disintegration of social order, culminating in a horrific civil war as the case of Sierra Leone, Liberia and Cote d'Ivoire. (The Ebola crisis is not mentioned here as the article was written in 2012. Nevertheless, it could be argued that its infectious spread is the result of a breakdown in health and social behaviours—a breakdown of good governance.) But the analysis should not stop there. Rather, it should also recommend common-sense civil solutions/measures that are respectful of the rule of law.

The question of behaviour—to be precise, negative behaviour- is one of the major stumbling blocks affecting development in post-colonial Africa. What do I mean by negative behaviour and how does it manifest itself? By negative behaviour, I'm talking about those attitudes, mind sets, practises, value systems and beliefs which emanate from culture and which, rather than promote constructive social relationships, disunite, or weaken the social fabric (well-being) of a nation. Often when planners (both external and internal) develop projects, most of the planning is focused on the supply side of development and for the most part the negative behaviour (values which are anaemic to transformational development-demand side) is not critically assessed. Maybe this is due to a paucity of Social Soundness Analysis; maybe it is driven by the urgency to implement projects.

Furthermore, negative social behaviour and attitudes might not appear important on the surface. Left unaddressed, however, they multiply to produce larger malignant problems. At the base of the problem is a fundamental lack of respect for civil or others' rights which are permutations of human rights. The notion that I'm my brother's keeper or what affects my brother affects me is absent. The following are six simple examples, drawn from my international development experience in several African countries. They are presented as simple examples of negative social behaviour for which solutions must be found.

Example 1:

My neighbour's sewer was leaking, and the waste ran past the entrance gate to the compound of my house. The leak caused a sanitation problem, as well as presenting a breeding site for mosquitoes. I brought the problem to the attention of my landlord who contacted my neighbour. The latter promised to do something but never did, and so the problem continued. Given the health hazard, I brought the problem to the attention of my Executive Officer who informed my landlord that if the problem was not solved in a month, my organisation would give up the house. I asked my landlord why he did not take the problem to the headquarters of the local commissariat to which he responded that doing so would, unfortunately, not solve the impasse. My landlord did not want to lose the financial remuneration received from my organisation. Accordingly, he decided to "solve" the problem himself. He had a pit dug on the outside of my neighbour's fence to allow the sewer to drain, thus stopping the flow past my entrance gate.

Example 2:

Another sewer problem of greater magnitude resulted in unsanitary leakage across a major thoroughfare in an "upscale" neighbourhood in the capital city. After my initial three years' service in this country, I was reassigned to it five years later. When I arrived for my second tour, I noticed that the problem had not yet been corrected. The situation had thus lasted for over five years. One of our drivers informed me that the leak came from a Minister's house and that the Minister could not care less. I could not understand why the Minister would not use his clout to address the problem that was causing a health hazard in the neighbourhood.

Example 3:

A transportation bus had a flat tire. While the tire was being changed, the passengers gathered on both sides of the road to eat their meals. Instead of collecting their refuse and putting it in a safe spot, they left it strewn all over the road to cause a sanitation hazard.

Example 4:

It is a common occurrence in several West African countries for drivers to park their cars on the sidewalks forcing pedestrians to walk on the street where they can be hit by cars. Even if you ask a driver to kindly park his car on the road, your request will be likely met by abuse; and if you insist you can be physically attacked. Requesting police enforcement is meaningless as they are easily bribed.

Example 5:

Car repairs on main roads are a common occurrence in several African countries. But once the car is repaired, be it replacing a punctured tire or fixing a problem that requires someone going underneath the car, the rocks used to hoist the vehicle are not removed from the road. Sometimes they are left in the middle of the road to pose a major hazard at night for other vehicles and pedestrians.

Example 6:

On a trip to monitor a project, the driver and I were in a discussion during which he mentioned his wife had dared to ask him how much he earned. He responded that he gave her a sound beating for having the impudence to ask him such a question, which was none of her business.

Discussion:

Respect for the rights of fellow human beings, expressed through the rule of law and civil behaviour/self-discipline, is pivotal to economic and social development - i.e., improving the quality of life. At its core, economic and social development require a behavioural change, one that enhances the human condition, rather than to subjugate it. Unfortunately, respect for "other's rights" (an extension of human rights) is absent in all the above examples, and the absence underscores the need for civility - which is a call for good governance. This process, acquired through civics and education, should start, in principle, from the home through primary school and continue through secondary education. In example 6, a political leader, with the temperament of the driver, would probably act in similar fashion against his opponents should he find himself in power someday. He would say, "How dare they question my authority?"

It is my contention that political and religious leaders, academics and civil servants (the intelligentsia) must make a concerted effort to investigate how such behaviours came about and whether they are linked to culture - in some countries these negative behaviours have been institutionalised to give rise to a way of life. Unfortunately, they have become the norm for ordering socio-economic interactions. In the absence of such an analysis, to be followed by the implementation of corrective measures, which should be nationally vetted, there is the strong likelihood of these negative behaviours returning to haunt the nation. Absence of the rule of law and civility is abundant in countries that have experienced social conflicts or countries described as "Fragile or Failed States." Not much has been done in my opinion to understand, on a national basis, what went wrong, how it went wrong, starting with a rigorous analysis of the colonial period, through independence and beyond, to pinpoint the stumbling blocks for which corrective measures need to be put in place. This type of rigorous analysing requires input from scholars interested in Africa - African and non-African. It is an analysis that should address the problems from within the African continent, an analysis, in the long-term, that should even start from the pre-colonial period.

In the short-term, however, these types of analysis should engage civil-society groups/community-based organisations operating at the grass-root level, the political structure, and should address those types of "minor problems" as described in the examples above. **It is my belief that it is from the successful results, emanating from the analyses of the minor problems, (i.e., the social**

structures), that, hopefully, the political will to address larger problems such as corruption, accountability, child-trafficking, good governance, etc., can be undertaken. It is also from these types of analysis that the economic and social well-being of the country can be enhanced, specifically putting in place the requisite building blocks for youth empowerment, a case in point. For this to take place concerted national leadership from all branches of government is of paramount importance.

Expected Results:

An expected result is laying the foundation for national dialogues at the grass root level that will engage citizens in civil-society debates on a continual basis. The idea is to bring citizens together to examine issues which affect the well-being of a community from a social, historical, and cultural context to arrive at common-sense solutions for establishing a social order that is respectful of civil rights and the rights of others. Since citizens have responsibilities to their communities, they must take ownership of their communities and be accountable, and by upholding the rights of others, members of a community are exercising their shared responsibilities to one another, thereby protecting a community's welfare - which is a requisite for good governance.

Another result is to establish a relationship in which aspects of the rule of law and the quality of social relationships serve as yardsticks for measuring national development/good governance. While national leaders are focused on nation building (i.e., economic, and social development), the African intelligentsia must be sensitive to behaviours that constantly undermine development and thereby affect the quality of life. Hopefully, by undertaking Operations Research i.e., Research designed to address issues arising from implementation - members of the intelligentsia will be able to identify how such negative behaviours develop; and feedback from such investigations should inform sensitive national discussions:

e.g. accountability, establishing codes of conduct for and declaration of assets of politicians, youth empowerment, land tenure, child trafficking, slavery, abuse of women, urbanization, etc.

It is only when the African Intelligentsia start to seriously analyse their political and cultural behaviours would they be able to postulate common sense solutions for addressing development matters.

APPENDICES

Appendix 1 - Classmates—Government Model School, 1949-52 (Standard 1-4)

1. Bunting *Bowen-Wright* (51) (Cub Scout) (went to the SLGS)
2. Modupe *Broderick* (49) (Cub Scout) (went to the POW)
3. Nicholas *Palmer* (49) (Cub Scout) (Went to the POW) (Deceased)
4. Lewis Tanimola *Pratt* (49) (Cub Scout) (Went to the POW)
5. Claudius *Campbell* (51) (Went to the MBHS) (Deceased)
6. Nqobisizwe Adekayode *Adetokumbo* (Richard Gordon Harris) (49) (Went to the POW)
7. Morley *Wright* (49) (Cub Scout) (Went to the SLGS)
8. Ernest *Nicol* (49) (Went to the SLGS)
9. Alfred *Sawyer* (49) (Cub Scout) ((Went to the SLGS)
10. Mohammed *Mahdi* (49) (Went to the POW) (Deceased)
11. Donald *Frazer* (49) (Cub Scout) (Deceased)
12. Chiquita *Noah* (49) (Went to MGHS) (Deceased)
13. Fredericka *John* (49)
14. Evelyn *Peters* (49)
15. Doreen *Macaulay* (49) (Went to AWMS)
16. Dalton *Macaulay* (49) (Cub Scout) (Went to the SLGS}
17. Cyril *Macaulay* (49) (Went to SE) (Deceased)
18. Crispin *Cross* (49) (Cub Scout) (Went to the POW}
19. Jemimah *Maddy* (50)
20. Winstina *Osho-Williams* (51)
21. Winston *Osho-Williams* (51)
22. Naib *Iscandari* (49) (Cub Scout) Went to the POW) (Deceased)
23. Gracie *Cole* (49) (Deceased)
24. Philip *Gage* (49) ((Went to the POW) (Deceased)
25. Willy *Grosvenor* (49) (Deceased)
26. Alfred *Harding* (51) (Went to the POW)

27. Henry *Cole* (51)
28. Lloyda *Davies* (49)
29. Richard (Roy) *During* (49) (Went to the AA)
30. Charles **Thornton** (51)
31. Godson *Leopold* (49) (Only did Standard One and left for Samaria School) (Went to the POW) (Deceased)
32. Rotimi *Paris* (50)
33. Prince *Doherty* (49)
34. Guilford *Jonah* (49)
35. Winifred Fijabi *Williams* (49)
36. Reginald *Horton* (49) (Deceased)
37. Iyamide *McCormack* (49)
38. Bamikole *Zubairu* (50) (Went to the SLGS)
39. Edwina *Meheux* (49)
40. Abu *Lamin* (50) Went to the POW) (Deceased)
41. Ebenezer *Fowler* (49) (Went to the POW) (Deceased)
42. Theodore *Gordon* (49) (Went to the POW) (Deceased)

The list of students below was provided by Bunting Bowen-Wright (The only person I recall from this list is Leonard Williams)

43. Papaboy *Taylor*,
44. Cosie *Taylor*
45. Samuel *Thorpe*
46. Annie *Doherty*
47. Leonard *Williams* (Went to the AA) (Deceased)
48. Arthur *Elliott*,
49. Willie *Elliott*
50. Samuel *Williams*

Our teachers:

Mr. Knox Macaulay (Headmaster)
Mr. Morgan (Succeeded Mr. Knox Macaulay as Headmaster)
Mr. Vincent
Mr. Fewry

Mr. Campbell
Mr. Gorvie (Scout Master)
Miss. Williams (Standard 1 and 2—1949 and 1950)
Miss. John (Standard 3--1951)
Miss. Johnson (Standard 4A--1952)
Mrs. Elliott (Standard 4B--1952)
Miss. Jarrett (Cub Mistress)

Appendix 2 - Photographs

Mama and Papa as a young couple

Broderick family at Brookfields in 1951

Mama in the 1930s

Mama as a young woman in the 1920s

Broderick ancestors 1890s

Papa portrait in 1960s in North Carolina

Papa & Mama as seniors

Modupe and Amelia at a West African post

Modupe and Amelia with their family – Christmas 2020

Modupe Broderick

Amelia Broderick

And our children

Ahovi Broderick

Vania Broderick Dursun

Proud Grandpa Modupe, with son Ahovi, and granddaughter Zara Dursun

Appendix 3: Letter of Commendation on Modupe's performance at the USAID Regional Office – Abidjan (REDSO)

UNITED STATES OF AMERICA
AGENCY FOR INTERNATIONAL DEVELOPMENT
REGIONAL ECONOMIC DEVELOPMENT SERVICES OFFICE WEST AND CENTRAL AFRICA

UNITED STATES ADDRESS
ABIDJAN (REDSO)
DEPARTMENT OF STATE
WASHINGTON, D. C. 20520

INTERNATIONAL ADDRESS
REDSO/WCA
C/O AMERICAN EMB.
01 B P 1712 ABIDJAN 0
COTE D'IVOIRE

May 25, 1990

Dr. Modupe Broderick
Program Specialist
CCCD Projet
REDSO/WCA
Abidjan, Cote d'Ivoire

LETTER OF COMMENDATION

Dear Dr. Broderick:

As I depart REDSO/WCA, I wish to commend you on your outstanding performance as Project Manager of the Combatting Childhood Communicable Diseases Project (CCCD). I arrived in REDSO/WCA in mid-1987 about the time you joined REDSO/WCA. The $1.6 million CCCD project was then considered to be in serious trouble and the technical backstop staff in AID/Washington and at the Center for Disease Control in Atlanta were on the verge of terminating it because of lack of progress. You immediately started to work on your arrival to improve our relations with the Ivorian Ministry of Health on all levels and you exercised exceptionally fine project management skills. Enough improvement occurred that a project evaluation made last year was able to recommend that the project not be terminated and it be given a little more time. Over the past year the fruit of all the past efforts became increasingly apparent. So much so, that as of this date the project has been completely turned around. Training activities are taking place. The Ministry of Health has become involved seriously improving the collection and dissemination of information. Vaccination programs are being strengthened. In the past week we inaugurated the Oral Rehydration Therapy Unit at the Treichville Hospital. It is off to a magnificent start as a treating and training unit for diarrheal disease control through oral rehydration therapy. I dare say it is one of the most handsome such units in Africa. Thanks to your rapport with ministry officials it is staffed up and functioning.

Your efficient, persistent, intelligent and sensitive management of this project has gained the admiration of everyone involved in it - AID/Washington, CDC/Atlanta and REDSO/WCA. Your exceptionally superb performance has been one of the key factors in making the project among the best and most

- 2 -

promising CCCD projects in Africa after being the opposite for several years before your arrival. I want to congratulate and commend you for this achievement and for your outstanding performance which made this possible.

I am requesting that a copy of this letter be put in your permanent personnel file.

Sincerely,

Arthur M. Fell
Director

Appendix 4 - Bibliography

Works Cited:

Bada, Myonnie. *Culture and Social Structures,* For Presentation at the 33rd Annual Internal Studies Convention, February 25 –March 1, 2003, isanet.ccit.arizona.edu/portlandarchives/bada.html

Ellis Island-"Free Port of New York Passenger Records Search," accessed March 7, 2013. http://www.ellisisland.org./view Text Manifest asp?MID=15554...

Fyle, Clifford and Eldred Jones, *A Krio-English Dictionary,* Oxford University Press and Sierra Leone University Press. 1980.

Kesteloot, Lilyan. Les ecrivains noirs de la langue francaise-naissance d'une literature, Bruxelles, l'institut de sociologie, 1963.

Koelle, Sigismund Wilhelm, Polyglotta Africana,AKADEMISCHE DRUCK-U, VERLAGSANSTALT, GRAZ-AUSTRIA, 1963.

Kopytoff, Jean Herskovits, *A Preface to Modern Nigeria: Sierra Leoneans in Yoruba, 1830-1890* Madison, MI: University of Wisconsin Press, 1965.

Lowther, Kevin G., *Odyssey of John Kizell*, University of South Carolina Press, Columbia South Carolina, 2011

Macauley, George James. Sierra Leone, Anglican (CNS) last modified?? Accessed October 24, 2013, http://www.dacb,org/stories/Sierra Leone/macauleygeorgejames,html.

Madison Area Committee on Southern Africa-African Activist," accessed September 15, 2013, http//Africa activist, mau.edu/organization.php?name-Madison+Area+Committee+on+Southern+Africa

"Somersett's Case," Wikipedia, last modified October 23, 2013, http//en.wikipedia.org/wiki:Somersett%-case#

Works Consulted:

Beaver, Philip, *AFRICAN MEMORANDUM: Relative to an Attempt to Establish a British Settlement on the Island of Bulama on the Western Coast of Africa, in the year 1792.* Negro University Press, Westport, Connecticut, 1970.

Caulker-Burnett, Imodale, *THE CAULKERS OF SIERRA LEONE: The Story of a Ruling Family and their Times,* Xlibris Corporation, United States of America, 2010.

Cole, Jibril R, THE KRIO OF WEST AFRICA, Ohio University Press, Athens, Ohio, 2013.

Hargrave, Carrie Guerphan, African Primitive Life...As I saw it in Sierra Leone British West Africa, Presses of Wilmington, North Carolina, 1944.

Hill, Lawrence, *The Book of Negroes*, Harper Collins, Canada, 2007.

Johnson, Omotunde, *Dancing with Trouble*, Langdon Street Press, Minneapolis, Minnesota, 2013.

Jones, Eldred Durosimi, *The Freetown Bond: A Life under Two Flags,* CPI Group (UK) Lid. Great Britain, 2012.

Karefa-Smart, John, Albert Musselman, *Rainbow Happenings: A Memoir,* Xlibris Corporation, United States of America, 2010.

Sanneh, Lamin, *Abolitionist Abroad,* Harvard University Press, Cambridge, Massachusetts, 2001.

Wade-Lewis, Margaret, *Lorenzo Dow Turner: Father of Gullah Studies,* University of South Carolina Press, Columbia South Carolina, 2007.

Compiled by the WLTF Literary Agency
www.winstonfordebooks.com